Series **3** | *Simon & Schuster's*

CROSTICS TREASURY

By

THOMAS H. MIDDLETON

A FIRESIDE BOOK
PUBLISHED BY SIMON & SCHUSTER INC.

New York   London   Toronto   Sydney   Tokyo   Singapore

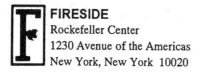

FIRESIDE
Rockefeller Center
1230 Avenue of the Americas
New York, New York 10020

The puzzles in this treasury have been previously published.
The puzzles in this volume have been selected from
Simon & Schuster Crostics 90, 91 and 92,
original copyright © 1983, 1984 by Simon and Schuster Inc.

Designed by Helen Barrow
Manufactured in the United States of America
10 9 8 7 6 5 4 3 2 1

ISBN: 0-671-87221-4

FOREWORD

Imagine being part of a gathering with this cast of characters: humorists, philosophers, doctors, scientists, comedians, journalists, poets, politicians . . . .

Where else would you find such a treat but in this "treasury" of Crostics inviting the solver to unearth 75 judicious and entertaining statements for fun and pleasure?!

THE PUBLISHER

COMPLETE ANSWERS WILL BE FOUND AT THE BACK.

JANUARY

S&S Hooked on Cryptics
Series #4

S&S Fun with Crostics
Series #8

FEBRUARY

S&S Crossword Puzzle Book
Series #177

MARCH

S&S Crostics Treasury #3

APRIL

S&S Crossword Puzzle Book
Series #178

MAY

S&S Large Type Crosswords
Series #17

JUNE

S&S Fun with Crostics
Series #9

S&S Crossword Puzzle Book
Series #179

JULY

S&S Crostics
Series #111

S&S Hooked on Puzzles
Series #7

AUGUST

S&S Crossword Puzzle Book
Series #180

SEPTEMBER

NEW! S&S Two-Minute Crosswords
Series #1

S&S Fun with Crostics
Series #1

S&S Fun with Crostics
Series #10

OCTOBER

S&S Fun with Crostics Treasury #1

S&S Crossword Puzzle Book
Series #181

NOVEMBER

S&S Crostics
Series #112

S&S Super Crossword Book
Series #8

DECEMBER

S&S Crossword Puzzle Book
Series #182

For puzzling pleasure year-round, treat yourself to the entire smorgasbord of Simon & Schuster crossword, cryptic, and crostic series—with fresh collections from Henry Hook, Eugene T. Maleska, Thomas H. Middleton, and John M. Samson, plus our very first *Fun with Crostics Treasury from Charles A. Duerr.*

And this year, we've added a new series to our puzzle calendar: *Simon & Schuster's Two-Minute Crosswords,* by crafty constructor David King. Designed to challenge even the speediest solvers, these inventive puzzles are a whole new concept in crosswords. You'll love them as much as you love the others.

No. 1

CLUES — **WORDS**

- **A** River of anc. Babylon — 89 76 132 214 153 174 231 112 8
- **B** 1910 Young-Olcott-Ball song from "Barry of Ballymore" (2 wds.) — 78 191 218 111 126 136 55 207 23 48 190 85
- **C** Housing for Flaherty's Nanook, e.g. — 50 146 177 149 115
- **D** "There shall be in England seven halfpenny ___ sold for a penny". ("Henry VI, Part 2") — 7 63 56 158 25 14
- **E** Stiff-growing annual herb of Mexico (hyph.) — 62 170 147 26 151 217 70 82 18 143 49 96 108 11
- **F** Business district. — 68 183 163 197 13 73 116 173
- **G** Cruel, barbarous. — 98 161 84 6 123 103 233
- **H** Gangs of witches — 12 135 209 3 164 138
- **I** Am. author (1885-1957; "Arundel"; full name) — 228 133 225 145 196 1 38 113 200 64 205 216 110 189
- **J** Particulars — 137 61 215 154 101
- **K** Seaport, NW Surinam (2 Dutch wds.) — 45 106 220 67 19 129 182 94 139 75 43 157 193
- **L** Formerly, 1/20th of a pound in England. — 83 95 60 10 199 52 192 117
- **M** Frequently. — 42 213 91 142 150 203 24 175 166 211
- **N** (Followed by WORD O) 1935 book by Anne Morrow Lindbergh. — 107 224 17 88 29
- **O** See WORD N (3 wds.) — 100 22 156 15 210 188 74 223 159 140 37
- **P** Brings a vessel to a standstill (2 wds.) — 33 141 180 51 30 4 219 232
- **Q** Bastard son of the Earl of Gloucester in "King Lear" — 152 127 131 34 20 40
- **R** 1916 Booth Tarkington novel. — 36 81 125 16 86 181 47 93 31
- **S** Depressed; ill (3 wds.) — 187 104 28 162 168 32 41 59 194 230
- **T** "Set me . . . as a seal ___: for love is strong as death" (3 wds.; "Song of Solomon, 8:5). — 121 102 58 77 35 186 227 184 39 128 134 171
- **U** Am. actor whose problems first publicly involved "palimony" (full name). — 208 202 229 72 109 66 80 144 179
- **V** Scat! beat it! — 21 195 99 124
- **W** Establish in a strong position — 234 122 65 97 120 53 198 46
- **X** Irish novelist and song-writer (1797-1868; "Rory O'More"). — 114 87 206 178 167
- **Y** Dr. L. L. Zamenhof's famous linguistic invention, introduced in 1887. — 69 90 148 54 169 172 221 212
- **Z** Coax. — 185 155 57 71 226 9
- **Z₁** Immediate divine illumination or wisdom. — 222 165 130 5 201 44 176 2 27
- **Z₂** Nearly cylindrical military cap — 105 92 118 160 79

No. 2

CLUES

A Province of SE Pakistan, cap. Karachi
B Coal scuttles
C Elaborates upon
D Friendly, cordial
E Wandering through
F In use; occupied the attention of
G Means of support
H Aromatic, myrtaceous tree of tropical America
I 1910 Victor Herbert operetta (2 wds.)
J Carl Sigman-Robert Maxwell song of 1953 (2 wds.)
K One who is made to bear the blame for another's mistake (2 wds.)
L Lather
M Secret benevolent society started in 18th-cent. England
N U.S. botanist and chemist (1864?-1943)
O Harmless
P Unyielding
Q Described
R Studying carefully; poring over; swindling
S Adorns
T Holmes beat him for the WBC heavyweight championship, 1978
U Sepulchers
V Commanding respect, reverence, etc.
W Lively
X Battle site, Am. Revolution, Jan. 17, 1781
Y Shopkeepers; artisans

WORDS

A 167 142 31 123
B 24 79 43 144
C 136 29 46 158 69 95 128 63 174 41
D 30 64 173 165 182 73 19
E 81 4 8 21 104 152
F 42 3 78 119 61 74 99 114
G 94 163 106 148 45 181 37 133 26
H 25 2 85 102 138 35 118 162
I 130 23 178 57 76 135 166 62 86 10 48 33 6 92 82
J 28 87 90 190 103 155 52
K 164 146 113 51 44 58 16 131 132 191 11
L 122 180 110 60
M 169 32 84 160 14 116 141 185 192 5
N 143 120 20 96 9 66
O 129 154 59 187 145 101 71 91 177
P 40 27 126 156 97 83 184
Q 47 55 125 151 39 186
R 22 175 56 68 15 109 170
S 157 38 189 1 67 105 72 168 50
T 36 65 161 172 80 13
U 75 88 112 140 107
V 89 124 115 12 139 100 70 111 179 149 171
W 108 193 150 18 153 134 77 54
X 49 147 188 93 159 53 121
Y 98 137 17 34 7 183 176 117 127

No. 3

CLUES / WORDS

	Clue	Word numbers
A	Pan, puss, mug	11 16 40 59 53 159
B	Accommodating, tolerant	45 70 19 87 28 22 47
C	Unaccommodating, intolerant	185 21 176 147 64 100
D	Dubbed	95 27 49 94 60 35 38 165
E	Kinship on the mother's side	86 33 94 60 35 38 164
F	Stupid, slow-thinking (hyph.)	71 41 4 180 12 80 36 79 145
G	Turkish saber	162 132 113 77 187 108 170 169
H	Relative of a schlemiel or a schlimazel	52 44 171 63 136 99 97
I	Kiln for drying hops or malt	30 84 137 151
J	Turkish title symbolized by horsetails	10 18 155 126 92 55 98 34
K	1923 Pulitzer Prize-winning play by Owen Davis	186 26 39 173 9 2 105 160
L	Gripped firmly	138 181 125 81 112
M	Pot, pool	85 104 15 189 73
N	Adj. describing most stained-glass windows	144 5 178 46 119 23
O	Anc. Gr. sculpture now in the British Museum (2 wds.)	93 130 116 51 149 3 25 69 57 143 128 14
P	"The ___ are wholesome; then no planets strike" ("Hamlet")	115 140 150 89 117 7
Q	Busy, active (3 wds.)	48 123 184 76 58 157 111 24 90
R	Thin, round pieces of food	20 142 96 107 124 158 1
S	Give concrete form to	82 156 50 177 43 174
T	Cruel, unrelenting, harsh	141 146 88 167 83 131 72 154
U	Foul condition; obscenity	62 114 17 8 188
V	Fatigue, exhaust; exaggerate	68 78 56 135 37 61
W	Mountain ash	133 74 67 183 122
X	Dull	103 32 166 54 153
Y	Disturbance of the heartbeat	172 6 127 182 65 152 102 29 161
Z	Cipher	42 91 75 106 118 120
Z_1	Taxi-drivers	134 163 175 110 101 121 13
Z_2	Spiny anteater	109 129 66 148 179 31 139

Diagram (cell number / clue letter, reading order)

Row 1: 1 R · 2 K · 3 O · 4 F · 5 N · 6 Y · 7 P · 8 U
Row 2: 9 K · 10 J · 11 A · 12 F · 13 Z_1 · 14 O · 15 M · 16 A · 17 U · 18 J · 19 B · 20 R · 21 C · 22 B · 23 N · 24 Q · 25 O · 26 K · 27 D
Row 3: 28 B · 29 Y · 30 I · 31 Z_2 · 32 X · 33 E · 34 J · 35 D · 36 F
Row 4: 37 V · 38 E · 39 K · 40 A · 41 F · 42 Z · 43 S · 44 H · 45 B · 46 N
Row 5: 47 B · 48 Q · 49 D · 50 S · 51 O · 52 H · 53 A · 54 X · 55 J · 56 V
Row 6: 57 O · 58 Q · 59 A · 60 E · 61 V · 62 U · 63 H · 64 C · 65 Y · 66 Z_2
Row 7: 67 W · 68 V · 69 O · 70 B · 71 F · 72 T · 73 M · 74 W · 75 Z
Row 8: 76 Q · 77 G · 78 V · 79 F · 80 F · 81 L · 82 S · 83 T · 84 I · 85 M
Row 9: 86 E · 87 B · 88 T · 89 P · 90 Q · 91 Z · 92 J · 93 O · 94 D · 95 D
Row 10: 96 R · 97 H · 98 J · 99 H · 100 C · 101 Z_1 · 102 Y · 103 X · 104 M · 105 K
Row 11: 106 Z · 107 R · 108 G · 109 Z_2 · 110 Z_1 · 111 Q · 112 L · 113 G · 114 U · 115 P
Row 12: 116 O · 117 P · 118 Z · 119 N · 120 Z · 121 Z_1 · 122 W · 123 Q · 124 R · 125 L
Row 13: 126 J · 127 Y · 128 O · 129 Z_2 · 130 O · 131 T · 132 G · 133 W · 134 Z_1
Row 14: 135 V · 136 H · 137 I · 138 L · 139 Z_2 · 140 P · 141 T · 142 R · 143 O · 144 N
Row 15: 145 F · 146 T · 147 C · 148 Z_2 · 149 O · 150 P · 151 I · 152 Y · 153 X
Row 16: 154 T · 155 J · 156 S · 157 Q · 158 R · 159 A · 160 K · 161 Y · 162 G · 163 Z_1
Row 17: 164 E · 165 D · 166 X · 167 T · 168 D · 169 G · 170 G · 171 H · 172 Y
Row 18: 173 K · 174 S · 175 Z_1 · 176 C · 177 S · 178 N · 179 Z_2 · 180 F · 181 L · 182 Y
Row 19: 183 W · 184 Q · 185 C · 186 K · 187 G · 188 U · 189 M

No. 4

CLUES

A Augmentation 125 98 40 168 143 119

B Russian violinist (1908-74) . . . 99 44 91 54 39 1 96 171

C Compassionate; causing sorrow or pity 5 36 170 159 97 62 155

D Cover up the defects of 42 65 163 48 139 127 47 20 89

E Spooky 120 165 92 13 123 105 45 31

F Instrument 'Omer smote (Kipling, "When 'Omer Smote") . . 26 157 58 116

G Seaport of Suffolk, Eng., famous for china 145 23 172 151 117 59 35 38 30

H Betides 49 154 34 81 53 87 104

I Easily decided (hyph.) 133 56 114 67 86 7 167 9 173 90 37

J Inaccuracy; fault 112 103 33 175 10 136 180

K Fr. physicist (1775–1836) after whom an electrical unit was named 32 100 150 166 71 160

L Slovenly, dirty 17 4 57 141 22 113

M Charged, commanded 70 161 52 142 50 179 137 102

N Middleton play based on a Machiavelli tale (2 wds.) 144 122 130 64 29 25 108 46

O "Round about the throne, were four beasts full ___ before and behind" (2 wds., Revelation 4:6) 73 162 68 82 128 11

P Poker-player's slang for "king" 85 61 177 138 111 72

Q Constant, unremitting 101 149 126 76 140 74 12 84 21

R Ballroom dance popular c. 1920 (hyph.) 79 28 6 55 110 148 77

S Observant; thoughtful 106 75 118 27 95 131 135 69 176

T Supple, limber 134 153 88 43 66

U He "proclaims that we live in the best of all possible worlds", while his opposite fears that it's true (Cabell, "The Silver Stallion") . . . 15 2 24 8 41 78 147 14

V No way! Never! (4 wds.) 124 3 63 83 51 115 132 80 93 18 178 16 109

W Branch of theology dealing with the promotion of peace 174 129 146 107 169 152 60

X As one desires (2 wds.) 19 121 158 94 156 164

No. 5

CLUES

WORDS

A Prophet returning aim after he settled in backward layer. 105 77 83 172 95 136 145 139

B I remove short cheroot so novel may emerge (2 wds., novel followed by WORD H). 81 12 176 96 154 141 144 9 160 65 3

C Dash against hard and long, unchecked. 20 71 85 94 1 19 119

D Wood spirit might be hotel man. . 5 91 76 28 21 150 161 166

E Public records bow to bees' homes 118 174 22 15 35 30 89 49

F Ordinal of a pain in the neck . . . 43 61 122 175 133

G Chart broken a long time in ancient city 147 129 162 108 115 86 40 69

H See WORD B (2 wds.) 8 64 102 14 158 78 121 112 128 41

I Luau, breaking up about five, leaves something on the roof of the mouth 127 90 124 138 63

J Teens we shake to make more agreeable. 80 135 104 116 125 157 171

K Purpose of a bivouac or circus? . 120 39 60 159 100 11

L Swelling, loud commotion in the Northeast 75 93 106 55 137 103

M Said way to date differently . . . 110 53 42 113 31 163

N Pressed, shut out, went ahead . . 156 84 131 57 66 51 88

O Broken main in whole, total agreement 25 117 140 111 38 70 99 114 67

P Plants with a thousand permits . . 54 18 92 59 148 132 48

Q Amen; but in the beginning it could be a sort of support 29 123 58 33 79 47 87 101

R Home in Tallinn, Estonia. 10 6 46 151

S Woman's place on the Arabian Peninsula. 153 17 173 52

T Pitches a patched potpourri . . . 7 44 34 98 109 146 13 169

U Transvestic role's blow is back East. 2 4 164 27 45 107 142

V In time, man without a heart could be threatening 32 62 24 74 37 73 130 143

W Anger in motion to the finish . . 134 82 165 23 36 72

X Cloud of bums in disarray 97 167 50 68 16 56

Y Close out badly after silence. Very loud (2 wds.) 26 126 149 155 170 168 152

No. 6

CLUES

A Leave in a difficult position . . . .

B 1722 Defoe novel (2 wds.) . . . .

C Hypothetical primitive language reconstructed by modern linguists (hyph.). . . . .

D Place in a difficult position . . . .

E Command indicating respect or approbation (2 wds.) . . . . . .

F Dissembled; equivocated; astounded . . . .

G "To crack a bottle with a friend / Or treat ___ men" (Chesterton, "Song Against Grocers"). . . .

H Turf. . . . .

I Pan, rap . . . .

J 1936 Robert E. Sherwood play (2 wds.) . . . .

K Not born yesterday (2 wds.). . . .

L "This ___, so variously foul" (3 wds.; Huxley, "Leda"). . . .

M "My murmuring rhyme / Beats with light wing against the ___" (2 wds.; William Morris, "The Earthly Paradise. An Apology").

N Anc. Phrygian city, home of Aeneas . . . .

O Hideous, rapacious winged monster with the head and body of a woman (Gr. myth.) . . . . . .

P Union general in the Civil War (1814-79) . . . .

Q Sharp change in attitude or opinion (hyph.). . . . .

R Thin, narrow strip of wood . . . .

S Fool around; waste time in aimless activity . . . .

T Huge, heavy, ungainly . . . .

U Tend, foster, treat, try to cure. . .

V Powers, potencies, intensities . . .

W Prompted; aroused . . . .

X Similarity in appearance of organisms belonging to different species . . . .

Y Walk, go, etc. . . . .

Z Pillage; torment. . . . .

WORDS

A	88	99	182	35	122	145						
B	43	83	107	37	42	118	189	187	5	143	68	59
C	151	1	94	103	168	148	57	64	185	139	21	115
D	52	102	167	132								
E	73	58	164	81	101	176	124					
F	3	165	16	162	175	63	49					
G	114	79	172	136	158	70	191	9	19			
H	152	28	14									
I	113	61	12	85	166							
J	171	181	117	193	149	163	109	93	48	121	55	24 95
K	87	60	97	41	71	120	156	177	96	128	160	
L	194	18	178	134	90	146	31	69	76	40	130	
M	89	8	135	154	6	188	15	11	67			
N	27	196	2	51								
O	138	157	137	184	30							
P	131	4	17	46	98	142						
Q	144	65	86	111	23	133	74	62	174			
R	125	78	72	106								
S	192	126	13	45	25	105	153	123				
T	7	119	33	141	100	54	82	127	80	129	161	
U	190	104	34	39	195							
V	66	75	92	20	112	36	84	53	26			
W	180	47	32	91	159							
X	186	140	56	155	179	22	169	150	44	173	77	
Y	116	10	183	147	50							
Z	170	38	29	110	108							

CLUES

A Incomprehensible talk (2 wds.) . . .

B Corruption . . . .

C Liveliness; specific pursuit . . . .

D Common metaphor for a recently elected group (2 wds.) . . . .

E Weakening . . . .

F Offer as a prize in a sort of gamble (2 wds.) . . . . . .

G Highest or farthest point . . .

H Affliction thought of as an act of God . . . .

I Under one's control or charge; being hauled (2 wds.) . . . .

J River that joins the Alabama River to form the Mobile River .

K Ornaments (metal) by engraving, embossing, etc. . . . . . .

L Fine and dandy, nifty, jake (hyph.) . . . .

M "He that ——, ruin meets" (2 wds.; Gay, "The Beggar's Opera") . . . .

N Rhizome . . . .

O Spelling according to accepted standards. . . . .

P Sudden, violent changes or disturbances . . . .

Q Undertaken or effected without the aid of others. . . . . .

R Rocket launch (hyph.) . . . . .

S Shunning; abstention. . . . .

T Madness . . . .

U Common honorary title, esp. in the South . . . .

V Showing; considering . . . . .

W Kampala is its capital. . . . .

X Comic effect produced by visual means (2 wds.) . . . . . .

Y Join by adhesion . . . .

Z Public show of feeling or opinion .

Z₁ "Near mournful / —— Paddington" (hyph.; Blake, "Jerusalem") . . . . . .

WORDS

A	18	27	169	159	46	212	56	93	137	188	6
B	190	38	179	173	235	222	42	234	102		
C	21	149	122	11	198	187	34	161			
D	53	148	100	116	209	73	184	134			
E	36	166	115	113	239	157	211	197	70	104	143	84
F	26	106	41	65	72	165	147	120			
G	152	25	92	172	83	199					
H	186	142	164	219	78	79	196	130	156	14	
I	44	192	228	215	51						
J	99	3	24	218	13	226	129	206	119		
K	109	181	61	136	175	153					
L	2	230	177	89	201	180	232	8	133	223	
M	96	111	95	163	17	59	35	202	174	195	185
N	91	58	114	1	140	60	178	183	110		
O	168	10	54	49	64	5	155	98	107	125	74
P	225	154	194	31	45	82	52	132	214		
Q	32	23	135	103	47	150	86	171	71		
R	238	29	66	189	9	146	40				
S	182	213	22	227	33	48	108	237			
T	210	69	28	145	118	16	221	158			
U	43	236	220	224	77	37	131				
V	205	76	216	138	117	167	233	7	88	12	
W	4	90	15	68	81	101					
X	123	19	144	97	229	127	208	231			
Y	139	112	240	160	67	124	128	176	217	57	204
Z	105	63	75	191	203	30	141	170	87	193	162	39	20
Z₁	85	62	126	200	151	241	55	94	121	80	207

No. 8

CLUES

A Ordinary · · · · · · · · · ·   49 7 191 136 10 131 74 104

B Where King John signed in 1215 · · · · · · · · ·   4 93 216 164 92 103 171 118 46

C "Instructed in geometry, that she might know something of the contagious countries," e.g. ("The Rivals") · · · · ·   70 37 178 53 85 57 22 208 26 140 9

D Secretary of the Treasury under Harding, Coolidge, and Hoover (1st and last names) · · · · ·   15 111 82 97 43 35 198 66 214 187 209 21

E Fought · · · · · · · · · ·   112 6 201 175 149 52 205

F "· · · a throne of royal state, which far / ___ the wealth of Ormus and of Ind" ("Paradise Lost") · · · · ·   19 31 217 170 142 114 68 34

G Works into a form or shape (Brit. sp.) · · · · · · · ·   36 113 169 75 64 42

H Courageous; presumptuous · · ·   65 177 212 102

I Outpouring · · · · · · · · · ·   8 181 203 80 55 1 135 27

J Graphs · · · · · · · · · · · ·   194 40 160 51 23 122

K Rejects, dismisses, sneezes at (2 wds.) · · · · · · · ·   54 195 210 13 121 108 71 132 18

L Speaks rapidly and unintelligibly · ·   148 154 14 24 120 152 207

M Destined to an unfortunate end (hyph.) · · · · · · · · · ·   150 60 81 2 211 73 158 17

N Fully extended; finally (2 wds.) · · ·   59 144 157 25 147 69 47 76

O "The ___ are wholesome; then no planets strike" ("Hamlet") · · ·   200 67 28 48 141 88

P In disorder · · · · · · · · · ·   84 134 12 153 91 96 119

Q Declining · · · · · · · · · ·   63 90 50 138 33 5

R Deceiving · · · · · · · · · ·   78 173 58 186 39 110 101 161

S Mountain in Thessaly · · · · ·   3 162 87 30

T Petroleum distillate used as a solvent, fuel, etc. · · · · · ·   16 215 139 176 172 190 204

U Approved, conventional · · · ·   41 72 115 145 168 156 182 193

V Interfere officiously · · · · · ·   184 197 95 155 32 130

W Faulkner county · · · · · · · ·   107 86 109 38 100 213 44 196 163 127 29 137 166

X Peewee · · · · · · · · · · · ·   98 167 183 56 125 116

Y Out front; winning (3 wds.) · · ·   206 83 99 11 77 188 185 174 165

Z 1911 Max Beerbohm novel (2 wds.) · · · · · · · · ·   62 117 133 192 89 151 128 105 123 159 180 202 94

Z₁ Noteworthy, remarkable, uncommon · · · · · · · ·   199 129 189 20 143 79 45 179 61 124 146 106 126

No. 9

CLUES — **WORDS**

- **A** 1847 ballad by E. A. Poe. 151 137 141 14 173 62 3
- **B** Followed by WORD K; type of knot (2 wds.) 75 6 11 92 134 26 121 71 21 44 152 117
- **C** Call to quarters 102 184 72 91 165 36
- **D** Temptation 154 100 187 28 181 59 86 93 111 1
- **E** Disorderly, unruly 41 90 153 172 147 189 80 178 110 113 124 140
- **F** Handled 50 175 65 74 190 85 38
- **G** In a group; altogether (2 wds.) . . 34 133 164 47 87 142 20
- **H** Self-styled radical activists of the late sixties and early seventies. . . 120 49 83 123 25 15 122
- **I** Bewitch 63 46 9 73 180 186 106
- **J** Cheers, supports (2 wds.) 4 168 156 13 139 114 31 56
- **K** See WORD B (2 wds.) 18 138 7 2 10 105 160
- **L** Disfigured, made less attractive . . 77 68 155 167 150 37 131 129
- **M** Disreputable; tawdry; vulgar. . . . 119 132 29 40 149 22 27
- **N** Number 3 wood. 61 115 52 84 162
- **O** Honorable 70 51 101 43 146 169 112 79 128 136
- **P** Ingenuity; falsehood 103 67 35 145 94 166 188 116 30
- **Q** Type of explosive device (2 wds.). 54 185 130 163 144 99 76 176
- **R** Kilns 159 42 78 182 60
- **S** Gushes 69 82 19 97 95 177
- **T** Knight, heroic champion. 183 81 58 127 157 66 12
- **U** Aquatic insectivore of W Africa (2 wds.) 39 104 118 8 53 17 89 125 57 23
- **V** Reverting of property to the lord of the manor when there are no legal heirs 5 16 98 24 126 143 148
- **W** Utter 88 45 96 55 171
- **X** Caused long-lasting resentment . . 179 170 135 109 48 107 33
- **Y** Prattle (hyph.). 158 64 32 161 174 108

1 D	2 K	3 A	4 J	5 V		6 B	7 K	8 U		9 I	10 K
11 B	12 T	13 J	14 A	15 H	16 V	17 U		18 K	19 S	20 G	21 B
22 M		23 U	24 V	25 H	26 B	27 M		28 D	29 M		30 P
31 J	32 Y		33 X	34 G	35 P	36 C	37 L	38 F		39 U	40 M
	41 E	42 R	43 O	44 B	45 W	46 I	47 G	48 X		49 H	50 F
51 O	52 N	53 U	54 Q		55 W	56 J	57 U		58 T	59 D	60 R
61 N		62 A	63 I	64 Y	65 F	66 T	67 P	68 L	69 S	70 O	71 B
	72 C	73 I	74 F	75 B		76 Q	77 L	78 R	79 O	80 E	81 T
82 S		83 H	84 N	85 F	86 D	87 G		88 W	89 U	90 E	91 C
	92 B	93 D	94 P	95 S		96 W	97 S		98 V	99 Q	100 D
101 O	102 C	103 P	104 U	105 K	106 I	107 X		108 Y		109 X	110 E
111 D	112 O		113 E	114 J		115 N	116 P	117 B	118 U	119 M	120 H
	121 B	122 H		123 H	124 E	125 U	126 V		127 T	128 O	129 L
	130 Q	131 L	132 M	133 G	134 B	135 X	136 O	137 A	138 K	139 J	140 E
	141 A	142 G		143 V		144 Q	145 P	146 O	147 E	148 V	149 M
150 L	151 A	152 B		153 E	154 D	155 L	156 J	157 T	158 Y		159 R
160 K		161 Y	162 N		163 Q	164 G	165 C	166 P	167 L	168 J	169 O
170 X	171 W		172 E	173 A	174 Y		175 F	176 Q	177 S	178 E	179 X
180 I	181 D	182 R		183 T	184 C	185 Q	186 I	187 D	188 P	189 E	190 F

No. 10

The diagram (an acrostic puzzle grid). Cells read left-to-right, each showing a number and its clue-letter:

1 B	2 I	3 N	4 R	5 D	6 P	7 V	8 O	9 M
10 H	11 S	12 N	13 R	14 R	15 R	16 Z₁	17 O	18 P
19 Y	20 N	21 K	22 X	23 L	24 W	25 S	26 Z	27 G	28 F
29 Q	30 Z₁	31 X	32 M	33 E	34 A	35 F	36 V	37 N
38 T	39 O	40 J	41 G	42 S	43 W	44 E	45 I	46 S
47 C	48 W	49 F	50 W	51 M	52 Z	53 C	54 O	55 E	56 Z₁
57 K	58 Z	59 Y	60 X	61 N	62 I	63 Z₁	64 T	65 Z	66 I
67 J	68 U	69 A	70 X	71 R	72 L	73 V	74 P	75 O	76 V	77 N
78 T	79 Q	80 C	81 R	82 V	83 G	84 E	85 C	86 A	87 D
88 O	89 I	90 V	91 S	92 Z	93 B	94 M	95 Z	96 U
97 V	98 J	99 B	100 Z	101 E	102 Z	103 A	104 Q	105 H	106 V
107 I	108 P	109 R	110 Q	111 A	112 Y	113 M	114 F	115 L
116 Z₁	117 O	118 J	119 A	120 V	121 E	122 Z₁	123 T	124 H	125 Y	126 K
127 V	128 P	129 Z₁	130 G	131 A	132 C	133 I	134 D	135 D	136 Z
137 I	138 B	139 Z	140 V	141 E	142 Y	143 O	144 H	145 U	146 U	147 I
148 T	149 S	150 G	151 R	152 Q	153 R	154 T	155 C	156 Z
157 G	158 K	159 V	160 X	161 C	162 K	163 T	164 C	165 Z₁
166 D	167 E	168 B	169 W	170 O	171 D	172 Y	173 R	174 C	175 W
176 F	177 T	178 M	179 U	180 L	181 Y	182 Z	183 O

CLUES

WORDS

Clue		Words
A	Mate	119 86 131 69 111 34 103
B	Tries the weight of	99 168 138 1 93
C	Nascent	174 132 155 47 164 80 85 53 161
D	Supple	87 166 171 5 134
E	Piscine	55 141 33 84 44 101 121 167
F	Units of illumination	176 49 114 35 28
G	Pickled	83 41 27 157 130 150
H	High balls of a sort	144 10 105 124
I	Mainstays (2 wds.)	62 66 107 2 137 89 133 45 147
J	First-rate; of the highest quality.	98 67 118 40
K	"An ampler ——, a diviner air" (Wordsworth, "Laodamia")	57 158 162 21 126
L	Exerts pressure and friction	115 180 23 72
M	Defeats, bests	94 178 51 113 32 9
N	Wife of Ahasuerus	37 61 12 77 3 20
O	Tender; with sentiment (Music)	143 88 170 75 8 39 117 54 183 17
P	Irish writer, painter, and songwriter (1797–1868; "Rory O'More").	108 128 74 6 18
Q	"—— trembled underneath her banks" ("Julius Caesar").	152 104 29 110 79
R	Raised with a jerk (2 wds.)	13 109 4 81 153 173 151 71 15
S	Declare, pronounce, attest	149 11 42 25 46 91
T	Put off	148 78 38 154 123 177 163 64
U	Lower; adulterate	179 96 68 146 145 14
V	Considering (4 wds.)	73 97 159 82 106 120 140 127 36 76 90 7
W	Frolics, bounds	48 50 24 169 175 43 116
X	Type of trunk	31 22 70 60 160
Y	Rudimentary, only begun	142 135 181 172 125 19 112 59
Z	Suddenly and unexpectedly (4 wds.)	26 65 136 156 139 182 95 52 102 58 92 100
Z₁	Apprehensive	63 122 165 129 16 30 56

CLUES

WORDS

A The least bit (informal). . . . . . | 143 73 26 119 177

B Timely . . . . | 6 77 159 172 176 122 82 34 96

C Fasten with cord . . . . . . | 124 126 133 87

D Unbroken . . . . | 161 181 55 140 110 47

E Extreme skeptic. . . . . . . | 168 54 163 134 144 12 184 108

F Dippy, nuts (hyph.). . . . . | 85 59 9 86

G One with unusually vivid mental images . . . . | 51 113 153 44 63 169 154

H Plaited frilling . . . . | 43 41 10 25 157

I Blemish. . . . . | 166 151 23 20 130

J Signify . . . . | 109 65 46 19 80

K Eliminates (2 wds.) . . . . . | 148 7 135 165 2 103 129 162

L Use . . . . | 118 100 139 78 49 182

M Opening line of Bulwer-Lytton's "Paul Clifford" (4 wds. followed by WORD O) . . . . | 167 120 160 142 107 123 38 42 70 95

N Eng. mathematician and physicist (1642-1727) . . . . . | 8 79 24 112 121 72

O See WORD M (3 wds.) . . . . | 94 179 83 98 15 147 58 156 39 37 106 30 11 92

P Desolate . . . . | 146 132 174 52 68

Q Eye-stalk, as in snails . . . . | 88 183 31 75 27 16 60 56 175 141 18

R Sure, yep, righto (hyph.) . . . | 64 125 138 5 149 180 3 32 21

S Evergreen shrub or small tree of the southern U.S. . . . . . . | 28 33 105 81 69 62

T What comes on the gravy train (2 wds.) . . . . | 145 61 97 178 76 40 173 53 136

U Distinguished . . . . | 115 99 17 36 127 89 131

V Long, detailed story . . . . . | 150 71 50 4

W Sycophants . . . . | 93 114 1 14 91 57 137

X Haggis ingredient . . . . . . | 22 111 170 67 90 45 13

Y Apparition. . . . . | 117 171 102 84 128 152

Z Prompt, speedy . . . . | 101 74 104 116 164 66 48 29 155 158 35

1 W	2 K	3 R	4 V	5 R	6 B	7 K	8 N	9 F
10 H	11 O	12 E	13 E	14 W	15 O	16 Q	17 U	18 Q
20 I	21 R	22 X	23 I	24 N	25 H	26 A	27 Q	28 S
29 Z	30 O	31 Q	32 R	33 S	34 B	35 Z	36 U	37 O
39 O	40 T	41 H	42 M	43 H	44 G	45 X	46 J	47 D
48 Z	49 L	50 V	51 G	52 P	53 T	54 E	55 D	56 Q
57 W	58 O	59 F	60 Q	61 T	62 S	63 G	64 R	65 J	66 Z
67 X	68 P	69 S	70 M	71 V	72 N	73 A	74 Z	75 Q
76 T	77 B	78 L	79 N	80 J	81 S	82 B	83 O	84 Y	85 F
86 F	87 C	88 Q	89 U	90 X	91 W	92 O	93 W
94 O	95 M	96 B	97 T	98 O	99 U	100 L	101 K	102 Y	103 K
104 Z	105 S	106 O	107 M	108 E	109 J	110 D	111 X	112 N	113 G	114 W	115 U
116 Z	117 Y	118 L	119 A	120 M	121 N	122 B	123 M	124 C
125 R	126 C	127 U	128 Y	129 K	130 I	131 U	132 P	133 Q	134 E
135 K	136 T	137 W	138 R	139 L	140 D	141 Q	142 M	143 A	144 E	145 T
146 P	147 O	148 K	149 R	150 V	151 I	152 Y	153 G	154 G
155 Z	156 O	157 H	158 Z	159 B	160 M	161 D	162 K	163 E
164 Z	165 K	166 I	167 M	168 E	169 G	170 X	171 Y	172 B	173 T	174 P
175 Q	176 B	177 A	178 T	179 O	180 R	181 D	182 L	183 Q	184 E

No. 12

CLUES

A O.K., passable (2 wds.) 134 96 46 136 27 4

B Anc. Greek beverage of wine and honey 62 84 164 151 32 158 139

C Drumbeat 83 52 113 104 35 6 161 75

D Inducement, drive. 132 106 141 40 126 99 86 18 117 162

E Combination, blend 45 159 38 26 93 43 64

F Beaks; points 103 31 10 143

G Yarns carried by the shuttle in weaving 116 140 152 39

H Large, flat-bottomed boats. 121 56 131 59 12

I What Hamlet says makes cowards of us all 172 138 42 50 23 120 160 89 97 150

J Characteristic of a wasting disease; characterized by rush, confusion, etc. 114 127 54 82 67 98

K Official, arbitrary decree or proclamation 11 66 145 19 123

L Answer 124 173 109 135 78 21 156 88 118

M Little whirlpools 36 30 108 154 15 137

N Large gray Indian antelope. 92 167 157 76 57 125

O Large hook used for landing large fish 9 49 129 63

P Grayish blue 105 3 87 74 29

Q Shackles 72 95 41 146 149

R Supports, reinforces 81 170 44 34 28 128 112

S Bold and resolute 48 20 130 5 61

T Was present 80 168 163 100 53 115 155

U Dozed, fell asleep (2 wds.) 68 110 122 107 25 119 94 2 153

V Asian tree with fan-shaped leaves and foul-smelling seeds 165 91 14 79 69 102

W Deficient 71 60 51 24 13 171 147

X Priceless 7 58 73 70 144 148 1 111 77 142

Y Long, tiresome speeches or writings 17 47 37 33 85 90 166

Z The Iberian Peninsula 55 22 16 169 65 8 101 133

WORDS / GRID

1 X	2 U	3 P	4 A	5 S	6 C	7 X	8 Z	9 O	10 F	
11 K	12 H	13 W	14 V	15 M	16 Z	17 Y	18 D	19 K	20 S	
21 L	22 Z	23 I	24 W	25 U	26 E	27 A	28 R	29 P	30 M	31 F
32 B	33 Y	34 R	35 C	36 M	37 Y	38 E	39 G	40 D	41 Q	42 I
43 E	44 R	45 E	46 A	47 Y	48 S	49 O	50 I	51 W	52 C	
53 T	54 J	55 Z	56 H	57 N	58 X	59 H	60 W	61 S	62 B	
63 O	64 E	65 Z	66 K	67 J	68 U	69 V	70 X	71 W		
72 Q	73 X	74 P	75 X	76 N	77 X	78 L	79 V	80 T	81 R	
82 J	83 C	84 B	85 Y	86 D	87 P	88 L	89 I	90 Y	91 V	92 N
93 E	94 U	95 Q	96 A	97 I	98 J	99 D	100 T	101 Z	102 V	
103 F	104 C	105 P	106 D	107 U	108 M	109 L	110 U	111 X	112 R	
113 C	114 L	115 T	116 G	117 D	118 L	119 U	120 I	121 H		
122 U	123 K	124 L	125 N	126 D	127 J	128 R	129 O	130 S	131 H	
132 D	133 Z	134 A	135 M	136 A	137 M	138 I	139 B	140 G	141 D	
142 X	143 F	144 X	145 X	146 Q	147 W	148 X	149 Q	150 I		
151 B	152 G	153 U	154 M	155 T	156 L	157 N	158 B	159 E	160 I	
161 C	162 D	163 T	164 B	165 V	166 Y	167 N	168 T	169 Z	170 R	171 W
172 I	173 L									

No. 13

CLUES

		WORDS
A	Shinbone.	171 145 96 86 213
B	Place of abode.	205 42 179 195 168 33 82
C	Ineffectual, bootless	207 143 2 187
D	Russ. composer and pianist (1873-1943).	32 106 200 26 43 71 13 170 65 97
E	"All heiresses are ——" ("King Arthur").	10 135 137 184 110 201 76 151 72
F	Coarse, opaque pottery.	102 70 5 182 130 161 177 90 7 158 59
G	Run-through.	155 12 160 67 91 41 44 29 56
H	Effective.	99 85 180 11 53 164 21
I	Gossip, rumor.	144 120 178 188 23 114 107
J	"O! that a man might know / The —— business, ere it come" (4 wds., "Julius Caesar"). . .	51 152 79 183 218 204 14 117 189 60 125 203 30
K	Fruit of the Spanish paprika. . .	69 17 196 209 181 192 159 169
L	Treated with malice.	146 197 211 50 154 186
M	"An attachment à la Plato for a bashful ——" (2 wds.; Gilbert, 'Patience'). . .	129 20 48 148 40 116 173 112 45 141 121
N	What Goldsmith's Lien Chi Altangi was "of the world". . .	153 167 73 35 212 133 185
O	Difficult, unpleasant situation to deal with (2 wds.). . .	28 216 221 55 61 94 191 64 100
P	Finesse.	157 176 24 132 215 202
Q	Popeye's "adoptik infink". . . .	66 25 206 81 37 89 83
R	Congress of Welsh bards and minstrels . . .	175 199 16 128 98 193 6 166 39 34
S	Olivia's steward ("Twelfth Night"). .	54 4 198 134 78 124 49 63
T	Stemless aquatic plant having sharp leaves.	9 58 19 80 131 223 214
U	Anonymity, obscurity.	87 150 105 111 163 136 75
V	One of the Gilbert and Ellice Islands, site of Nov., 1943, U.S. victory. .	208 219 38 95 108 104
W	Gradually (3 wds.)	22 149 119 88 162 46 127 93 139 138
X	Air-supply control on an internal-combustion engine . . .	220 74 18 84 165
Y	Study of fishes	1 123 172 190 113 15 77 210 27 101 57
Z	Talks back.	194 147 52 92 118 174
Z₁	Device for compressing a blood vessel.	115 36 140 126 217 142 47 68 3 103

Diagram

1 Y	2 C	3 Z₁	4 S	5 F	6 R	7 F	8 D	9 T		
10 E	11 H	12 H	13 C	14 J	15 Y	16 R	17 K	18 X	19 T	20 M
21 H	22 W	23 I	24 P	25 Q	26 D	27 Y	28 O	29 G	30 J	
31 D	32 D	33 B	34 R	35 N	36 Z₁	37 Q	38 V	39 R		
40 M	41 M	42 B	43 D	44 G	45 M	46 W	47 Z₁	48 M	49 S	
50 L	51 J	52 Z	53 H	54 S	55 O	56 G	57 Y	58 T	59 F	
60 J	61 O	62 D	63 S	64 O	65 D	66 Q	67 G			
68 Z₁	69 K	70 F	71 E	72 E	73 N	74 X	75 U	76 E		
77 Y	78 S	79 J	80 T	81 Q	82 B	83 Q	84 X	85 H		
86 A	87 U	88 W	89 Q	90 F	91 G	92 Z	93 W	94 O		
95 V	96 A	97 C	98 C	99 H	100 O	101 Y	102 F	103 Z₁		
104 V	105 U	106 D	107 I	108 V	109 D	110 E	111 U	112 M	113 Y	
114 I	115 Z₁	116 M	117 J	118 Z	119 W	120 I	121 M	122 D		
123 Y	124 S	125 J	126 Z₁	127 W	128 R	129 M	130 F	131 T	132 P	133 N
134 O	135 E	136 U	137 E	138 W	139 W	140 Z₁	141 M	142 Z₁		
143 C	144 I	145 A	146 L	147 Z	148 M	149 W	150 U	151 E	152 J	
153 N	154 L	155 G	156 D	157 P	158 F	159 K	160 G	161 F		
162 W	163 U	164 H	165 X	166 R	167 N	168 B	169 K	170 C	171 A	
172 Y	173 M	174 Z	175 R	176 P	177 F	178 I	179 B	180 H	181 K	
182 F	183 J	184 E	185 N	186 L	187 C	188 I	189 J	190 Y	191 O	192 K
193 R	194 Z	195 B	196 K	197 L	198 S	199 R	200 D	201 E	202 P	203 J
204 J	205 B	206 Q	207 C	208 V	209 K	210 Y	211 L	212 N	213 A	
214 T	215 P	216 O	217 Z₁	218 J	219 V	220 X	221 O	222 D	223 T	

No. 14

CLUES — **WORDS**

Clue		Word numbers
A	Prong, cog	30 71 102 62 129
B	Nuptial poem by Spenser	98 160 165 29 12 34 115 19 56 90 6 177
C	Retributive justice	7 88 175 23 153 158 18
D	1928 Romberg opera (2 wds. after *The*)	172 13 86 69 139 3 109
E	Rube	111 123 125 97 161
F	Mitigate, tone down	107 122 163 83 37 150
G	Demosthenes, Cicero, etc.	147 40 170 61 180 140 79
H	Aura	127 68 159 114 10 50
I	Am. author (1876–1916; "Martin Eden")	58 21 28 128 113 75
J	Degradation	144 119 60 134 87 103 93 112 117
K	Title formerly given to some Portuguese and Brazilian dignitaries	182 173 138
L	"Nine-and-twenty ___ tall" (Scott, "Lay of the Last Minstrel")	5 59 85 44 27 82
M	Punish; purify, refine	80 31 154 100 95 39 17
N	Long, thin slip of wood	66 135 91 169
O	Bowed, curved	45 89 65 143 78 36
P	Wheel with many a WORD A	174 131 168 146 84 104 101
Q	Missing	43 92 96 120 38 152
R	Authoritative prohibition	15 137 142 149
S	1895 novel by Theodor Fontane (2 wds.)	64 1 72 52 26 132 49 16 55 166
T	Highest part	148 181 108 53
U	Behaved theatrically	141 4 74 133 32 42
V	Bill, score, bad news	156 176 99 164 121 54 25
W	Small herb of the high Alps	81 47 116 110 51 11 126 70 157
X	Home of dead Teutonic heroes	22 14 179 63 9 73 41
Y	An "Athens of the North"	151 124 94 155 8 24 35 76 48
Z	Joshing, putting on	136 57 20 178 106 145 33
Z_1	Mercy "is ___ in the hearts of kings," says Portia ("Merchant of Venice")	130 171 105 167 2 118 46 162 77

No. 15

CLUES

		WORDS
A	Repeated alternation	24 84 109 149 120 197
B	Removes (2 wds.)	38 93 63 6 141 129 131 158 237
C	Trollope novel (2 wds. after *The*)	133 73 124 147 205 227 100 51 56 154 168 152 92 70 118
D	Outrageously base or wicked	215 114 43 59 88 140 221 231 10 32
E	Live the life of Riley, roll in clover (5 wds.)	165 37 235 204 230 74 113 151 119 5 45 132 216 217 138 146
F	Shot in the dark, conjecture (2 wds.)	18 78 130 101 65 30 136 159 11 209 127 176 57
G	Constructed in layers	199 214 121 218 193 31 13 23 34
H	"The stateliest measure ever moulded by the ___" (3 wds.; Tennyson, "To Virgil")	190 175 178 137 236 171 164 69 206
I	Give additional or fuller treatment	161 200 53 28 91 8 107 229 17
J	Large lake trout of northern North America	41 103 108 167 97 87 226 46 184
K	"The Fighting ___" (1943 film with Dennis O'Keefe)	62 29 233 160 82 55 170
L	Aristophanes' specialty	25 40 16 189 105 21
M	Excessively proud and arrogant (hyph.)	14 4 194 68 182 232 22 1 198 142 157 80 61
N	Unwholesomely gloomy	54 96 102 7 39 225
O	Searching stealthily (3 wds.)	125 155 203 81 224 58 173 15 3 94
P	Richly picturesque	36 181 210 163 48 111 86 153
Q	Stab; cleave through	150 106 67 166 33
R	Grassy surface, turf	238 112 49 180 85
S	Advocacy, defense; first place	115 75 60 219 179 44 9 145 123 195 117 188
T	Sermon, admonitory discourse	99 64 126 27 191 2
U	Shakespearean play that features Beatrice and Benedick (4 wds.)	135 122 162 116 42 156 110 228 201 148 169 76 134 186 98 174 90 139 213
V	Unusual (4 wds.)	72 35 95 143 208 185 12 212 20 26 50 177 83 223
W	Type of paving material	183 79 71 47 222 196 187 19 172 52 202
X	Wise guy (hyph.)	207 104 220 211 144 89 77 234 66

Grid (cell number / letter)

1 M	2 T	3 O	4 M	5 E	6 B					
7 N	8 I	9 S	10 D	11 F	12 V	13 G	14 M	15 O	16 L	17 I
18 F	19 W	20 V	21 L	22 M	23 G	24 A	25 L	26 V		
27 T	28 I	29 K	30 F	31 G	32 D	33 Q	34 G	35 V	36 P	
37 E	38 B	39 N	40 L	41 J	42 U	43 D	44 S	45 E	46 J	
47 W	48 P	49 R	50 V	51 C	52 W	53 I	54 N	55 K	56 C	
57 F	58 O	59 D	60 S	61 M	62 K	63 B	64 N	65 F	66 X	
67 Q	68 M	69 H	70 C	71 W	72 V	73 C	74 E	75 S	76 U	
77 X	78 F	79 W	80 M	81 O	82 K	83 V	84 A	85 R	86 P	
87 J	88 D	89 X	90 U	91 I	92 C	93 B	94 O	95 V	96 N	97 I
98 U	99 T	100 C	101 F	102 N	103 J	104 X	105 L	106 Q		
107 I	108 J	109 A	110 U	111 P	112 R	113 E	114 D	115 S	116 U	
117 S	118 J	119 E	120 A	121 G	122 U	123 S	124 C	125 O		
126 T	127 F	128 V	129 B	130 F	131 B	132 E	133 C	134 U		
135 U	136 F	137 H	138 E	139 I	140 D	141 B	142 M	143 V		
144 X	145 S	146 E	147 C	148 U	149 A	150 Q	151 E	152 C	153 P	
154 C	155 O	156 U	157 M	158 B	159 F	160 K	161 I	162 U		
163 P	164 H	165 E	166 Q	167 J	168 C	169 U	170 K	171 H	172 W	
173 O	174 U	175 H	176 F	177 V	178 H	179 S	180 R	181 P	182 M	
183 W	184 J	185 V	186 U	187 W	188 S	189 L	190 H	191 T	192 V	
193 G	194 M	195 S	196 W	197 A	198 M	199 G	200 I	201 U		
202 W	203 O	204 E	205 C	206 H	207 X	208 V	209 F	210 P	211 X	
212 V	213 U	214 G	215 D	216 E	217 E	218 G	219 S	220 X		
221 D	222 W	223 V	224 O	225 N	226 J	227 C	228 U	229 I	230 E	231 D
232 M	233 K	234 X	235 E	236 H	237 B	238 R				

No. 16

Grid

The grid cells (each showing its number and the clue-letter it belongs to):

1 O	2 D	3 A	4 Z	5 W	6 B	7 C	8 Y	9 P	10 R
11 T	12 A	13 X	14 T	15 X	16 P	17 A	18 D	19 W	20 S
21 Q	22 L	23 R	24 G	25 C	26 K	27 J	28 X	29 V	30 I
31 X	32 J	33 E	34 G	35 D	36 S	37 O	38 H	39 R	40 P
41 K	42 L	43 Y	44 W	45 D	46 G	47 Z	48 S	49 H	50 C
51 U	52 B	53 E	54 I	55 Z	56 M	57 D	58 U	59 Q	60 J
61 H	62 B	63 S	64 K	65 T	66 G	67 U	68 S	69 D	70 G
71 J	72 Z	73 S	74 U	75 U	76 H	77 X	78 L	79 E	80 T
81 J	82 D	83 P	84 B	85 A	86 I	87 M	88 Y	89 N	90 C
91 P	92 G	93 X	94 P	95 E	96 R	97 L	98 J	99 K	100 Z
101 X	102 S	103 R	104 F	105 O	106 M	107 C	108 N	109 J	110 D
111 J	112 Q	113 N	114 J	115 I	116 X	117 V	118 K	119 D	120 O
121 O	122 K	123 V	124 E	125 B	126 P	127 Z	128 P	129 R	130 W
131 B	132 U	133 K	134 G	135 S	136 R	137 D	138 O	139 E	140 A
141 B	142 E	143 P	144 G	145 Q	146 X	147 T	148 V	149 F	150 S
151 N	152 O	153 K	154 D	155 R	156 C	157 Z	158 B	159 M	160 D
161 K	162 F	163 Z	164 Y	165 Q	166 X	167 O	168 Q	169 Z	170 Y
171 V	172 H	173 F	174 B	175 U	176 A	177 T	178 Q	179 R	180 S
181 H	182 F	183 I	184 P	185 L	186 E	187 B	188 U	189 N	190 B

CLUES / WORDS

A Essence; phantom; zeal 17 3 85 140 176 12

B Dominating 125 84 158 6 190 187 131 62 174 52 141

C Dutch colonial administrator in America (1580–1638) 107 156 90 25 7 50

D Aberration 69 154 45 35 82 110 137 119 57 160 18 2

E Without aim or purpose 33 79 124 95 139 186 142 53

F Thick slices 162 182 104 149 173

G Optional 92 134 70 24 144 66 34 46

H Large-billed tropical American bird 172 181 61 38 49 76

I Minute dipterous insect 54 115 30 86 183

J Predetermined, arranged, set . . . 98 60 114 111 81 109 27 32 71

K Aberrant 133 41 161 153 118 64 99 122 26

L Heartache 42 97 185 78 22

M Female red deer 106 87 56 159

N Semilegendary fabulist 89 108 113 189 151

O Manager of the Yankees, 1931–46 . . . . 167 105 121 37 152 120 1 138

P Intimate association or relation . 91 16 94 184 40 83 143 128 126 9

Q Intentional slight; insult 178 21 112 165 168 59 145

R Gull with a very short or rudimentary hind toe 39 23 103 155 10 179 96 129 136

S Faint illumination on the part of the moon not lit by the sun . . . 102 73 36 135 180 63 48 20 68 150

T Feels, discerns 80 65 147 11 14 177

U Assistant 58 132 188 75 67 51 74 175

V Sap, dolt, numskull 171 117 123 29 148

W Cut into small cubes 19 44 5 130

X Wife of Hector and mother of Astyanax 28 31 101 116 146 15 93 77 13 166

Y Bathes 88 164 43 170 8

Z Emanation from the body of a medium 100 157 47 4 163 127 55 72 169

CLUES

WORDS

Clue		Numbers
A	Am. playwright ("The Price"; full name)	167 18 54 131 173 150 47 81 39 90 148 104
B	Remarkable	198 25 16 92 130 60 45 100 74 72
C	Embroidery, e.g.	187 129 179 91 215 165 109 82 1 40
D	Compound reciprocal pronoun (2 wds.)	76 118 172 158 125 194 64 67 206
E	Start, flinch	157 213 31 53 36
F	Flat, round, leavened cakes	29 105 111 160 196 42
G	Feelings, emotions	161 135 212 203 186 71 147 80
H	Uninteresting, pointless	103 180 79 141 209 41 35
I	Iterative sound of beating	205 52 57 176 21 3 10 128
J	Affording passage by vessels	115 106 136 191 183 28 175 200 117
K	Captivated by (2 wds.)	190 5 164 178 153 63 146 87 139
L	Pertaining to a Judaic sect founded in Poland in the 18th cen.	59 162 202 14 185 23 95
M	Surrounds, envelops; suburbs	120 8 93 193 70 210 86 108
N	Zero, zilch, scratch (2 wds.)	156 22 199 15 201 171 145 181
O	Dried muscats, e.g.	163 182 127 24 154 144 61
P	TV rabbit-ears, perhaps	38 159 177 78 50 126
Q	Duty of the fortunate to be charitable (2 Fr. wds.)	26 85 214 116 140 124 149 56 98 112 133 195 9 75
R	Complexities	7 155 168 114 34 189 123 84 48 137 97
S	"'Tis distance lends enchantment to ___" (2 wds.; Campbell, "Pleasures of Hope")	69 110 17 192 204 62 37
T	Card game usually played with the 32 highest cards in the deck	143 113 11 101 174 134
U	European wild cherry trees	27 216 43 49 6
V	Eng. poet (1880–1958; "The Highwayman"; full name)	32 51 20 107 4 66 13 89 55 96 208
W	Boasts, brags	142 132 121 19 77 30 99 169 12 166 2 68
X	Sprinkling with powder	119 151 33 58 46 83 122
Y	Bristly, prickly	184 44 170 94 211 188 73 102
Z	Wisest of the Greeks in the Trojan War	152 207 197 138 65 88

No. 18

CLUES

Clue		Word numbers
A	Modest	12 16 51 92 107 163
B	Aircraft propelled by flapping wings	22 173 95 43 122 129 28 80 65 74 142
C	Undulations	111 132 37 151 83
D	Father of Aeneas	94 149 135 118 40 6 87 154
E	Italian seaport on the Adriatic	159 108 131 112 146 1
F	Ancestry	144 42 82 34 157 50 165
G	Prattles, blathers, spouts off	110 64 86 178 119 11
H	Fullness; scope or breadth	91 115 45 39 19 102 148 31 63
I	Without restraint; dissolute	32 176 55 54 166 96 85
J	Types of papers	62 61 21 30 100 172 125
K	Tyro	9 49 58 134 73 79
L	Cover or surround with something solid	141 53 124 168 103 26
M	Substance used for polishing metals	46 81 128 162 68 14 97 175 77 60 38
N	Secure	167 161 139 113 84 23
O	Attain	56 71 127 150 66
P	Result, consequence	106 41 70 130 90 93 153 3 156
Q	Encounter	126 59 5 20 36 78 158
R	Divert	57 109 117 143 99 155 137 13 2
S	Range	18 140 33 105 101
T	Oriental concubine	147 104 8 170 123 48 15 29 174
U	Lacking force, weak	76 169 121 177 27 17 88
V	Great sources of supply	44 10 25 145 164
W	As a stopgap (3 wds.)	75 138 116 7 47 72 98 4
X	Oriental name meaning "Comfort of God"	69 160 171 35 120 136 89 114
Y	Is foolishly fond	152 24 133 52 67

WORDS (grid)

Row	Cells
1	1 E · 2 R · 3 P · 4 W · 5 Q · 6 D
2	7 W · 8 T · 9 K · 10 V · 11 G · 12 A · 13 R · 14 M · 15 T · 16 A · 17 U
3	18 S · 19 H · 20 Q · 21 J · 22 B · 23 N · 24 Y · 25 V · 26 L · 27 U
4	28 B · 29 T · 30 J · 31 H · 32 I · 33 S · 34 F · 35 X · 36 Q · 37 C · 38 M
5	39 H · 40 D · 41 P · 42 F · 43 B · 44 V · 45 H · 46 M · 47 W · 48 T
6	49 K · 50 F · 51 A · 52 Y · 53 L · 54 I · 55 I · 56 O · 57 R · 58 K
7	59 Q · 60 M · 61 J · 62 J · 63 H · 64 G · 65 B · 66 O · 67 Y
8	68 M · 69 X · 70 P · 71 O · 72 W · 73 K · 74 B · 75 W · 76 U · 77 M
9	78 Q · 79 K · 80 B · 81 M · 82 F · 83 C · 84 N · 85 I · 86 G · 87 D · 88 U
10	89 X · 90 P · 91 H · 92 A · 93 P · 94 D · 95 B · 96 I · 97 M · 98 W
11	99 R · 100 J · 101 S · 102 H · 103 L · 104 T · 105 S · 106 P · 107 A · 108 E · 109 R
12	110 G · 111 C · 112 E · 113 N · 114 X · 115 H · 116 W · 117 R · 118 D · 119 G
13	120 X · 121 U · 122 B · 123 T · 124 L · 125 J · 126 Q · 127 O · 128 M · 129 B · 130 P
14	131 E · 132 C · 133 Y · 134 K · 135 D · 136 X · 137 R · 138 W · 139 N · 140 S · 141 L
15	142 B · 143 R · 144 F · 145 V · 146 E · 147 T · 148 H · 149 D · 150 O · 151 C · 152 Y
16	153 P · 154 D · 155 R · 156 P · 157 F · 158 Q · 159 E · 160 X · 161 N
17	162 M · 163 A · 164 V · 165 F · 166 I · 167 N · 168 L · 169 U · 170 T
18	171 X · 172 J · 173 B · 174 T · 175 M · 176 I · 177 U · 178 G

CLUES   WORDS

A Laying it on thick, soft-soaping · 128 200 153 29 170 181 41

B Muse of comedy and lyric poetry · 155 102 94 133 137 187

C Am. novelist (1862-1937); "The House of Mirth"; full name) · 182 158 35 74 80 204 194 106 115 101 184 98

D Parti-colored · 7 39 20 14 166 140 62

E Expression of exasperation or disbelief · 146 126 175 203 119 63 8 124

F 1861 novel by Mrs. Henry Wood that became an immensely popular melodrama (2 wds.) · 118 148 192 202 165 10 45 142 105

G Anc. capital of Assyria · 207 87 51 42 167 61 136

H Central, cardinal · 78 31 57 110 178 1 164

I Canadian city called Bytown until 1854 · 76 132 100 161 189 85

J "There's no sweeter ___ comes from Virginia" (Thackeray, "The Virginians") · 172 67 123 130 17 11 65

K Alarm bell · 72 114 54 99 44 13

L Am. author and poet (1809-49; "To Helen", "The Bells"; full name) · 81 23 90 197 160 27 104 188 144 183 145 55 15

M 1912 song by William Jerome and Jimmie V. Monaco (3 wds.) · 147 73 135 205 91 64 152 180 75

N Grasping, rapacious · 37 59 150 186 40 25

O 1934 Cole Porter musical (2 wds.) · 96 36 48 193 117 19 71 208 143 201 108 26

P Thomas Bulfinch's field · 154 134 139 30 159 47 50 89 191

Q Irregular, peculiar · 195 116 6 22 69 60 109 49 52

R Ready and delicate in reaction · 138 103 127 4 97 33 177 21 157

S Portuguese territory in S China · 198 12 125 112 174

T 1964 Arthur Miller play (3 wds.) · 16 151 43 163 121 129 179 53 111 9 34 84

U Taking small bites · 131 173 2 24 92 70 82 95

V Forces crudely, coerces · 149 122 88 66 162 168 46 196

W Progress · 156 58 171 107 176 3 86

X Very much, very badly (4 wds.) · 5 56 120 18 199 68 206 169 32 185 79 190 28

Y Black-and-white sea bird of northern regions · 83 77 38 93 141 113

1 H	2 U	3 W	4	5 R	6 X	7	8 E	9 T	10 F
11	12 S	13 K	14 D	15 L	16 T	17 J	18 X	19 O	
20 D	21 R	22 Q	23 K	24 U	25 N	26 O	27 L	28 X	29 A
30 P	31 H	32 X	33 R	34 T	35 C	36 O	37 N	38 Y	39 D
40 N	41 A	42 G	43 T	44 K	45 F	46 V	47 P	48 O	49 Q
50 P	51 G	52 Q	53 T	54 K	55 L	56 X	57 H	58 W	59 N
60 Q	61 G	62 D	63 E	64 M	65 J	66 V	67 J	68 X	69 Q
70 U	71 O	72 K	73 X	74 C	75 M	76 I	77 Y	78 H	
79 X	80 C	81 L	82 U	83 Y	84 T	85 I	86 W	87 G	88 V
90 L	91 M	92 U	93 Y	94 B	95 U	96 O	97 R	98 C	99 K
100 I	101 C	102 B	103 R	104 L	105 F	106 C	107 W	108 O	109 Q
110 H	111 H	112 S	113 Y	114 K	115 C	116 Q	117 O	118 F	
119 E	120 X	121 X	122 V	123 J	124 E	125 S	126 E	127 R	128 A
129 T	130 J	131 U	132 I	133 B	134 P	135 M	136 G	137 B	138 R	139 P
140 D	141 Y	142 F	143 O	144 L	145 L	146 E	147 M	148 F	149 V
150 N	151 T	152 M	153 A	154 P	155 B	156 W	157 R	158 C	
159 P	160 L	161 I	162 V	163 T	164 H	165 F	166 D	167 G	168 V	169 X
170 A	171 W	172 J	173 U	174 S	175 E	176 W	177 R	178 H	179 T
180 M	181 A	182 C	183 L	184 C	185 X	186 N	187 B	188 L	189 I
190 X	191 P	192 F	193 O	194 C	195 Q	196 V	197 L	198 S	199 X
200 A	201 O	202 F	203 E	204 C	205 M	206 X	207 G	208 O	

No. 20

CLUES

		WORDS
A	Whiter whale minced for money . . .	192 88 7 148 79 21 40 135 1 89 123
B	Everything expand? That's all right (2 wds.) . . .	151 43 122 178 128 70 194 19
C	Beat a gentle creature to a bad set . .	160 170 3 6 80 51 30 186
D	Play went last, held up following WORD B (3 wds.) . . .	74 141 25 83 207 163 153 118 14 159 42 187
E	Offer to start making attempt. . . .	37 69 169 110 57 181
F	First principles of misturned debacle.	32 143 61 167 198 157 139 209 90
G	Cord easily handled as a boat surrounded by land.	113 103 64 173 22 137 66
H	Puts out of commission captaincies at work.	67 5 29 189 206 65 134 174 120 124 140 150 177
I	Minesweeper's dance about sun-god .	45 31 180 56 146 100 190 17
J	Terror of holding up an ice-house. . .	34 60 152 162 172
K	May's past with, most important, full vigor (3 wds.).	156 129 78 99 115 200 50 105 95 4 154
L	Dogmatic verse, as it comes out . . .	77 185 166 147 126 39 114 16 179
M	Minor switched 500 to hunter.	93 138 199 47 20 82
N	Support in hours in trouble	81 136 86 108 117 182 53
O	Snack fit in return to piscine appendage	36 164 132 188 63 171
P	One who's been to Mecca had joined in beginnings.	84 112 202 27 8
Q	Nature of scene's collapse after excellent beginning	15 109 149 46 73 196 204
R	Dogface to measure present	10 104 68 184
S	Hudson village of song is in trouble .	13 102 101 121 130 193 23 87
T	"An ill wind that no one blows good," sang Danny Kaye.	35 26 85 72 28
U	French town's demise: its Jacquerie overthrew nobility initially. . . .	24 75 91 127 201
V	Sits holding semi-high spots.	98 145 131 12 165 119
W	Groan about liver, perhaps.	197 71 125 176 111
X	Old tax concession's heart	208 107 94 155
Y	I meant strangely confined one	183 38 59 92 97 28
Z	Giving royal eye: men's alterations . .	33 195 58 142 76 49 11 44 168 133 158 55
Z₁	Pus appears? (2 wds.).	52 96 203 144 48 2 106
Z₂	Dry eyes at recollecting the past	116 54 205 175 62 18 191 41 161

No. 21

CLUES

WORDS

A Sophocles tragedy (2 wds.) 138 119 92 70 105 59 208 29 33 35

B Fasteners. 164 214 22 147 3 88 184

C Erstwhile name of Ghana's neighbor (2 wds.) 67 140 93 200 161 110 169 81 87 39

D Confirm 27 142 148 48 64 155

E Considered, thought; valued . . .   181 198 213 51 34 78 62 190

F Remember 7 195 120 63 216 172 19 163 150

G Agrees (with) (2 wds.) 101 207 8 11 165 193

H Manipulative type of person 129 18 180 12 134 203 77 98 103

I 1900 Conrad novel (2 wds.) 108 47 204 13 58 177 1

J "She dwelt among the untrodden ways / Beside the springs of ___" (Wordsworth) 60 44 206 160

K Kit and caboodle, shooting match . .   86 115 42 107 24 210 5

L "My very noble and approv'd good ___" ("Othello"). 196 55 187 90 28 132 50

M Fat chance! Like fun! (4 wds.) 173 197 154 133 209 72 185 146 82 84

N Forest-land. 168 122 176 83 126 128

O Transmitted in line of descent. . . .   74 91 53 116 194 158 69 16 96 30

P Not settled (4 wds.). 106 117 135 189 14 23 37 6 141 89

Q Emergencies 127 97 46 152 145 183 76

R Equip. 192 52 21 94 215 174

S Sydney is its capital (3 wds.) 123 79 54 49 15 179 144 9 143 66 171 112 17

T Struggle, usu. with some success . . .   36 31 202 26

U Contrite 2 186 65 167 136 73 85 32 102

V Impeccable; artless 118 182 71 4 43 131 100 114

W Skinflint 40 151 61 125 113 95 201 211

X Belong intrinsically 149 68 41 212 20 121

Y Ammunition chest 191 57 109 159 175 205 45

Z At all (3 wds.) 99 178 25 157 162 153 104 188 111 124

Z₁ "Just when we're ___; there's a sunset-touch" (Browning, "Bishop Blougram's Apology") 156 170 139 75 56 137

Z₂ Clears away; disposes of what's left of the enemy (2 wds.) 80 199 38 166 10 130

No. 22

CLUES

A. 1933 film, first of the Astaire-Rogers musicals (4 wds.)
B. Immediate apprehension
C. Who lives "in this heart of mine" in a 1928 song by Harris and Young (2 wds.)
D. Blurred effect at the edges of a light area of a photograph
E. Demanded, required
F. Hyde Park equestrian path (2 wds.)
G. Convert into a like substance, as food in the body
H. Boutiques, e.g.
I. "Scorning ___ / By which he did ascend" (3 wds., "Julius Caesar")
J. Nazi to whom Hitler dictated "Mein Kampf"
K. 1598 Ben Jonson comedy
L. Unbridled, unrestrained
M. Considering (4 wds.)
N. Tirelessly, unceasingly (3 wds.)
O. Grublike females of certain beetles, family Lampyridae
P. Kakapo (hyph.)
Q. Let
R. Dumbfounded; staggered
S. They are split by Goat Island, in western N.Y. State (2 wds.)
T. Give a vitreous coating to
U. In stir; in the big house (3 wds.)
V. Eating and drinking
W. Rascal
X. Words of the same spelling but different pronunciations and meanings
Y. "Thou Soul that art the ___," (3 wds.; Wordsworth, "The Prelude")
Z. Volcanic mountain in the Cascade Range, California

WORDS

A. 243 111 103 51 215 182 137 64 39 80 125 86 85 124 20
B. 140 134 213 122 156 131 240 55 94
C. 108 197 88 127 101 119 152 133
D. 22 66 178 208 143 99 107 149
E. 192 130 220 63 153 223 95
F. 171 24 54 67 199 147 245 84 232
G. 12 221 227 118 169 5 50 166 97 158
H. 196 78 151 237 18
I. 11 229 37 43 226 161 74 59 30 53 139 136 163 167
J. 42 144 188 6
K. 26 194 214 228 132 3 117 160 58 246 87 218 79 114 34 155 69 62 195 106
L. 49 15 202 225 44 159 168
M. 146 241 17 177 201 224 210 19 29 231 121 46
N. 211 185 77 61 191 116 128 145 157 238 179
O. 70 222 65 33 204 23 92 105 41
P. 126 9 209 135 200 112 186 89 173 96
Q. 165 187 57 73 207
R. 181 162 48 72 21 32 13 100 109
S. 56 76 110 242 142 123 170 104 230 164 193 36
T. 217 4 82 184 68
U. 71 138 176 198 236 31 83 233 205
V. 148 16 212 203 38 2 216 113 175
W. 1 60 91 102 93 47 234 154
X. 45 28 206 8 52 40 172 239 174 81
Y. 189 7 244 25 150 75 247
Z. 115 27 183 120 219 35

No. 23

CLUES / WORDS

A. Encloses; hits 37 50 90 121 114

B. Proposition or scheme for peace. .   108 6 171 207 69 40 36 206 147

C. One of the Hawaiian Islands 103 58 201 169 138 52 185

D. Wide-spouted pitchers 173 149 134 155 168

E. Affirmation by negation of the contrary 187 210 78 57 136 95 67

F. Hatred of women 94 35 113 12 123 175 19 166 178 75

G. Morbid fear of open places   54 153 16 92 208 25 101 143 186 73 196

H. However, yet 129 15 26 27 60 209 119 184 74 46 8 55 62 197 31

I. Man thought to be masterful and irresistibly charming to women .   49 127 80 176 110

J. Most ill-tempered and scrappy .   51 191 18 7 87 157 120 63 106

K. That can be reached, entered, etc. 200 96 130 102 72 82 28 79 156 117

L. "Guilty creatures sitting at a play / Have by the very cunning of ____" (2 wds., "Hamlet") . . .   167 152 131 183 56 161 204 189

M. Mind; notice 43 24 5 84

N. "By ____ to-morrow / Thou must be made immortal" ("Measure for Measure") . .   93 179 20 160 211

O. "The Red Baron" (1892-1918).   107 66 158 88 205 133 9 193 188 122

P. Small, aquatic, egg-laying monotreme of Australia and Tasmania (hyph. and wd.) .   48 38 23 59 53 146 111 124 139 13 181 174 154 199 162 64 163 105

Q. Supplement; make up the required measure (2 wds.) . . .   112 145 172 182 81 151

R. Self-evident 203 22 86 68 180 97 177 150 142

S. Rhizome 33 65 194 91 77 1 141 109 17

T. "Would I had met my dearest ____ in heaven" ("Hamlet") . .   170 11 165

U. Civility, courtesy 115 100 118 83 47 140 202 144 192

V. 1890 poetic drama by Paul Claudel (English title; 2 wds.). .   61 30 99 14 198 42 135

W. Am. industrialist and political leader (1822-1903) who married Peter Cooper's daughter 2 44 85 125 159 39

X. Outfielder for the Cards, 1938-53; nicknamed "Country" (full name) 21 41 128 126 164 34 137 71 10 45 132 3 195

Y. What you'll find yourself in, according to Irving Berlin's "Easter Parade" (after *the*) 98 70 29 104 148 4 32 190 76 116 89

Diagram

1 S	2 W	3 X	4 Y	5 M	■	6 B	7 J	8 H	9 O	■
10 X	11 T	12 F	13 P	14 V	15 H	16 G	17 S	18 J	19 F	20 N
21 X	22 R	23 P	24 M	25 G	26 H	■	27 H	28 K	29 Y	30 V
31 H	32 Y	33 S	34 X	35 F	36 B	■	37 A	38 P	39 W	■
40 B	41 X	42 V	43 M	44 W	■	45 X	46 H	47 U	48 P	49 I
50 A	51 J	52 C	■	53 Q	54 G	55 H	56 L	57 E	■	■
58 C	59 P	60 H	61 V	62 H	63 J	64 P	65 S	66 O	■	■
67 E	68 R	69 B	70 Y	71 X	72 K	■	73 G	74 H	75 F	76 Y
77 S	78 E	79 K	80 I	81 Q	82 K	83 U	84 M	85 W	■	■
86 R	87 J	88 O	89 Y	90 A	91 S	92 G	93 N	94 F	95 E	■
96 K	97 R	98 Y	99 V	100 U	101 G	102 K	103 C	104 Y	105 P	■
106 J	107 O	108 B	109 S	110 I	111 P	112 Q	113 F	114 A	115 U	■
116 Y	117 K	118 U	119 H	120 J	121 A	122 O	123 F	124 P	125 W	■
126 X	127 I	128 X	129 H	130 K	131 L	132 X	133 O	134 D	135 V	■
136 E	137 X	138 C	139 P	140 U	141 S	142 R	143 G	144 U	■	■
145 Q	146 P	147 B	148 Y	149 D	150 R	151 Q	152 L	153 G	154 P	■
155 D	156 K	157 J	158 O	159 W	160 N	161 L	162 P	163 P	164 X	■
165 T	166 F	167 L	168 D	169 C	170 T	171 B	172 Q	173 D	■	■
174 P	175 F	176 I	177 R	178 F	179 N	180 R	181 P	182 Q	183 L	■
184 H	185 C	186 G	187 E	188 O	189 L	190 Y	191 J	192 U	193 O	■
194 S	195 X	196 G	197 H	198 V	199 P	200 K	201 C	202 U	203 R	■
204 L	205 O	206 B	207 B	208 G	209 H	210 E	211 N	■	■	■

No. 24

CLUES

		WORDS
A	Deputy	101 5 142 67 19 114 65 28 97 133 129 54 94 141
B	Unmindful	98 173 11 40 179 136 29 48
C	Attack from concealment	102 172 71 45 55 80
D	Hideous	122 64 27 56 53 178 190
E	Ending of two successive clauses with the same word, in rhetoric	182 44 169 146 79 31 137 82 42 15
F	A medusa	125 107 118 63 134 95 62 72 33 18
G	Levy of one-tenth	162 113 151 123 14
H	Criteria of scarcity (2 wds.)	147 89 16 104 17 186 181 41 57
I	Wreathe	32 96 196 13 7 39 131
J	Deal heavy blows	10 116 192 128 165 6
K	Deep-seated; private	85 158 75 117 148 124 175 199
L	Alert, wary (4 wds.)	77 168 184 120 155 115 135 198 110 164 81
M	Stuffed shirts, perhaps	34 150 58 69 109
N	Turkish title of respect	119 138 2 43 52 126 74
O	Able to withstand drought	183 159 26 111 66 171 157 60 61 195
P	Derange	167 103 87 47 144 92 194
Q	Invincible	38 189 88 197 105 49 25 76
R	Natives of Riga, e.g.	73 191 91 12 170
S	Gala	78 51 86 100 121 154 188
T	Materials needed to win a fight, support an argument, etc.	161 187 8 143 90 152 22 1 23 174
U	Thin, fine clothing fabric	21 4 177 193 24 36 84
V	"By the pricking of my ___" ("Macbeth")	3 140 83 50 180 108
W	Presumptuous, arrogant	68 132 149 156 176 9 99 112 163 46 30
X	Type of bank entitlements (2 wds.)	106 145 166 70 185 93 20 37 59 127 160 130 139 153

No. 25

CLUES

A. Constraining or cementing forces 17 75 65 177 30

B. Impermeability to radiant heat 139 13 170 86 62 106 118 152 193 82

C. Unwilling 79 161 6 117 124 103 189 59 169

D. Australian weaver-bird striped black and gray (2 wds.) 204 115 14 40 81 22 216 60 52 188

E. Thicken, condense 175 165 129 211 151 83 90 186 147 61

F. Very large, intelligent breed of dog 220 48 174 74 123 55 190 77 25 58 120 80

G. Fixed into a surrounding mass 145 88 69 212 191 43 138 127

H. Quarrel (2 wds.) 54 3 32 109 219 89 121

I. Withstands 99 42 221 203 9 26 132

J. Unreservedly 178 11 71 8 93 49 200 133

K. Hodgepodge 29 128 154 172 160 141 12 181

L. Laughs (wd. coined by Lewis Carroll) 185 156 96 207 215 18 39 176

M. Hero killed by Paris 51 95 134 70 126 187 108 198

N. Summer 105 72 143 218 97 195 84 5

O. Bland firecrackers 140 116 210 192 202 63

P. "Wherefore with thee / Came not / broke loose?" (2 wds.; Milton, "Paradise Lost") 16 76 122 114 28 167 183

Q. Those who work for or urge change, esp. political 194 208 100 159 2 179 201 50 112

R. "I saw him fumble with —— and play with flowers" (2 wds., "Henry V") 1 104 15 214 47 173 182 146 162

S. Inspection 73 110 149 213 4 119 24 150

T. "So doth the greater glory dim / Venice")" (2 wds., "Merchant of 197 130 23 148 157 35 41

U. "He saith among the trumpets, Ha, ha; and —— the battle afar off" (2 wds., Job 39:25) 27 7 94 38 153 137 144 19 217 85

V. Fairylike creatures 131 56 33 78 107

W. Decayed; out of fashion (hyph.) 57 21 199 158 31 68 180 98 45

X. Dispositions 125 155 171 44 20 164 66 53 209

Y. Incited, provoked 196 101 37 111 142 113 135 92

Z. Mean, signify 36 10 163 168 206 91

Z₁ Druggist 205 136 184 46 67 34 166 64 102 87

WORDS

1 R	2 Q	3 H	4 S	5 N	6 C	7 U	8 J	9 I		
10 Z	11 J	12 K	13 B	14 D	15 R	16 P	17 A	18 L	19 U	
20 X	21 X		22 D	23 T	24 S	25 F	26 I	27 U	28 P	
29 K	30 A	31 W	32 W	33 V	34 Z₁	35 T	36 Z	37 Y	38 U	39 L
40 D	41 I	42 I	43 G	44 X	45 W	46 F	47 Z₁	48 F		
49 J	50 Q	51 M	52 D	53 D	54 H	55 E	56 V	57 W	58 F	59 C
60 D	61 E	62 B	63 O	64 Z₁	65 A	66 X	67 Z₁	68 W	69 G	
70 M	71 J	72 N	73 S	74 F	75 A	76 P	77 F	78 V	79 C	
80 F	81 D	82 B	83 E	84 N	85 U	86 B	87 Z₁			
89 H	90 E	91 Z	92 Y	93 J	94 U	95 M	96 L	97 N	98 W	99 I
100 Q	101 Y	102 Z₁		103 C	104 R	105 N	106 B	107 V	108 M	109 H
110 S	111 Y	112 Q		113 Y	114 P	115 D	116 O	117 C	118 B	119 S
120 F	121 H	122 P	123 F	124 C	125 X	126 M	127 G	128 K	129 E	
130 T	131 V	132 I	133 J	134 M	135 Y	136 Z₁	137 U	138 G	139 B	
140 O	141 K	142 Y	143 N	144 U	145 G	146 R	147 E	148 T	149 S	
150 S	151 E	152 B	153 U	154 K	155 X	156 L	157 T	158 W	159 Q	
160 K	161 C	162 R	163 Z	164 X	165 E	166 Z₁	167 P	168 Z	169 C	170 B
171 X	172 K	173 R	174 F	175 E	176 L	177 A	178 J	179 Q		
180 W	181 K	182 R	183 P	184 Z₁	185 L	186 E	187 M	188 D	189 C	
190 F	191 G	192 O	193 B	194 Q	195 N	196 Y	197 T	198 M	199 W	200 J
201 Q	202 O	203 I	204 D	205 Z₁	206 Z	207 L	208 Q	209 X	210 O	
211 E	212 G	213 S	214 R	215 L	216 D	217 U	218 N	219 H	220 F	221 I

No. 26

CLUES

A. Am. writer (1888–1959), creator of Philip Marlowe (full name) · · · · · · · · · ·
B. Furnishing with power, authority, etc. · ·
C. Popular cocktail accompaniments · · · · ·
D. Hampered, thwarted · · · · · · · · · · ·
E. Defense, justification · · · · · · · · · · ·
F. Indulging in unrestrained revelry or other disorderly behavior · · · · · · · · · · ·
G. Diminish; fall asleep (2 wds.) · · · · · · ·
H. Overflowing with water · · · · · · · · · ·
I. Brutal, violent person · · · · · · · · · · ·
J. Young children; rag dolls · · · · · · · · ·
K. Brother of Electra and Iphigenia · · · · ·
L. Grasp, realize · · · · · · · · · · · · · · ·
M. About ·
N. Badge, mark · · · · · · · · · · · · · · · · ·
O. "The breath of _____" (hyph. & wd.; Theodore Dreiser, "The Banks of the Wabash") · ·
P. Desert in E Asia · · · · · · · · · · · · · ·
Q. Fastened · · · · · · · · · · · · · · · · · · ·
R. Producing no effect · · · · · · · · · · · · ·
S. "The resident Djinn, / Number _____, Simmery Axe!" (Gilbert, "The Sorcerer") · · · · ·
T. Men's singles winner, Wimbledon, 1956–57 · ·
U. Slow passage in music · · · · · · · · · · ·
V. Complex · · · · · · · · · · · · · · · · · · ·
W. Young slave in "Uncle Tom's Cabin" · · ·
X. Settle ·
Y. Devotee, fan · · · · · · · · · · · · · · · · ·
Z. Privations · · · · · · · · · · · · · · · · · ·
Z₁. Japanese art of flower arrangement · · · ·
Z₂. Eng.-born Am. novelist ("The Captains and the Kings"; full name) · · · · · · · · · · ·

WORDS

Clue	Letters (grid numbers)
A	11 20 168 211 77 86 91 60 89 133 158 151 33 45 47
B	170 67 83 40 134 163 35 186 4
C	37 187 140 98 123 118 192
D	15 174 127 71 101 38 27
E	22 122 16 181 161 148 160
F	166 202 185 64 145 96 110
G	50 144 69 177 105 201 152
H	138 156 93 176 143
I	162 190 200 175 184 10 82
J	73 112 63 100 8 104 173
K	66 154 108 204 76 3 197
L	25 36 12 107 210 75 167 49 70 126
M	128 153 180 87 55 196 139
N	79 171 59 32 53 206
O	85 52 209 31 92 5 95 159 62 130 56
P	58 48 137 39 199 208 26 111 129 84
Q	103 150 74 44
R	146 29 54 179 164 90 94
S	106 81 7 117 78 183 34
T	28 121 135 207
U	18 178 124 142 72
V	57 102 88 43 165 198 6 1 172
W	114 149 30 19 9
X	61 24 189 212 21
Y	131 203 155 2 194 13 65 182 113 191
Z	119 17 68 46 157 80
Z₁	51 193 42 188 115 116 141
Z₂	41 205 120 136 99 23 14 109 147 97 132 125 195 169

Grid (number — letter)

1 V	2 Y	3 K	4 B	5 O	6 V
7 S	8 J	9 W	10 I	11 A	12 L
13 Y	14 Z₂	15 D	16 E	17 Z	18 U
19 W	20 A	21 X	22 E	23 Z₂	24 X
25 L	26 P	27 D	28 T	29 R	30 W
31 O	32 N	33 A	34 S	35 B	36 L
37 C	38 D	39 P	40 B	41 Z₂	42 Z₁
43 V	44 Q	45 A	46 Z	47 A	48 P
49 L	50 G	51 Z₁	52 O	53 N	54 R
55 M	56 O	57 V	58 P	59 N	60 A
61 X	62 O	63 J	64 F	65 Y	66 K
67 B	68 Z	69 G	70 L	71 D	72 U
73 J	74 Q	75 L	76 K	77 A	78 S
79 N	80 Z	81 S	82 I	83 B	84 P
85 O	86 A	87 M	88 V	89 A	90 R
91 A	92 O	93 H	94 R	95 O	96 F
97 Z₂	98 C	99 Z₂	100 J	101 D	102 V
103 Q	104 J	105 G	106 S	107 L	108 K
109 Z₂	110 F	111 P	112 J	113 Y	114 W
115 Z₁	116 Z₁	117 S	118 C	119 Z	120 Z₂
121 T	122 E	123 C	124 U	125 Z₂	126 L
127 D	128 M	129 P	130 O	131 Y	132 Z₂
133 A	134 B	135 T	136 Z₂	137 P	138 H
139 M	140 C	141 Z₁	142 U	143 H	144 G
145 F	146 R	147 Z₂	148 E	149 W	150 Q
151 A	152 G	153 M	154 K	155 Y	156 H
157 Z	158 A	159 O	160 E	161 E	162 I
163 B	164 R	165 V	166 F	167 L	168 A
169 Z₂	170 B	171 N	172 V	173 J	174 D
175 I	176 H	177 G	178 U	179 R	180 M
181 E	182 Y	183 S	184 I	185 F	186 B
187 C	188 Z₁	189 X	190 I	191 Y	192 C
193 Z₁	194 Y	195 Z₂	196 M	197 K	198 V
199 P	200 I	201 G	202 F	203 Y	204 K
205 Z₂	206 N	207 T	208 P	209 O	210 L
211 A	212 X				

No. 27

CLUES

		WORDS
A	Filch; suitable	46 86 183 84 71 131 136 150 103 28 56
B	Liberated, unrestrained	122 158 5 156 67 177 163 206 200 126
C	Brackets for candles; heads	92 188 203 72 176 153 51
D	Aswarm, prolific	6 148 12 82 171 95 102
E	Natural impulses	187 59 108 21 157 141 193 70 27
F	Unfavorable renown	107 65 50 174 87 52 205 31 85
G	1955 Jules Dassin film	80 124 75 133 110 145
H	Food or drink of the Greek gods.	138 208 99 24 196 179 81 159
I	Knotty point; complication	45 106 11 184 53
J	Purely intellectual	112 42 115 211 105 62
K	Likenesses of a person	23 89 40 101 197 64 128 20
L	Town NW of Rouen, France, once a monarchy whose king was the subject of a song by Béranger	170 204 36 192 19 146
M	Immeasurably extended in time and space	166 143 49 18 61 155
N	1952 Western written by Carl Foreman, directed by Fred Zinnemann (2 wds.)	77 35 202 181 16 94 58 2
O	Secretary	69 123 130 210 43 182 125 147 93 172
P	Mixture of preserved fruits, nuts, etc., used as a dessert sauce (3 wds.)	154 162 139 117 8 10 44 109 17 73
Q	Fair-to-middling, at best (3 wds.)	30 98 76 91 165 55 9 180
R	Huge, clumsy	119 186 137 79 7 191 66 152 26 114 135
S	Rhythmic cadence	97 121 34 14
T	Because	189 48 207 57 168
U	Right away (3 wds.)	88 142 37 173 68 127 185 15 54
V	Overflows	160 100 140 74 120 164
W	"And I in ___ for the heat, / To drink there" (D.H. Lawrence, "Snake")	22 111 41 175 134 178 13
X	Made too great demands on	39 60 209 144 104 83 149 33 195
Y	Sagacity, discernment	190 167 38 129 198 118
Z	Am. actress and singer ("Cabin in the Sky"; "Member of the Wedding"; full name)	78 63 194 29 47 116 96 169 3 201 151
Z₁	Juvenile series by Edward Stratemeyer (2 wds after The)	132 1 199 90 161 32 4 113 25

Grid

1 Z₁	2 N	3 Z	■	4 Z₁	5 B	■	6 D	7 R	8 P	
9 Q	10 P	11 I	12 D	13 W	14 S	15 U	16 V	17 P	18 M	
19 L	20 K	21 E	22 W	23 K	24 H	25 Z₁	26 R	27 E	28 A	29 Z
30 Q	31 F	32 ■	33 Z₁	34 S	35 N	36 L	37 U	38 Y	39 X	
40 K	41 W	42 J	43 O	44 P	45 I	46 A	47 Z	48 T	49 M	50 F
51 C	52 F	53 I	54 U	55 Q	56 V	57 T	58 N	59 E		
60 X	61 M	62 J	63 Z	64 K	65 F	66 R	67 B	68 U	69 O	70 E
71 A	72 P	73 P	74 V	75 Q	76 Q	77 N	78 Z			
79 R	80 G	81 H	82 D	83 X	84 X	85 A	86 A	87 F	88 U	89 K
90 Z₁	91 Q	92 C	93 O	94 N	95 D	96 Z	97 S	98 Q	99 H	100 V
101 K	102 D	103 A	104 X	105 J	106 I	107 F	108 E	109 P	110 G	
111 W	112 J	113 Z₁	114 R	115 J	116 Z	117 P	118 Y	119 R	120 V	
121 S	122 B	123 O	124 G	125 O	126 B	127 U	128 K	129 K	130 O	
131 A	132 Z₁	133 G	134 W	135 R	136 A	137 R	138 H	139 P	140 V	
141 E	142 U	143 M	144 X	145 G	146 L	147 O	148 D	149 X		
150 A	151 Z	152 R	153 C	154 P	155 M	156 B	157 E	158 B	159 H	
160 V	161 Z₁	162 P	163 B	164 V	165 Q	166 M	167 Y	168 T	169 Z	
170 L	171 D	172 O	173 U	174 F	175 W	176 C	177 B			
178 W	179 H	180 Q	181 N	182 O	183 A	184 I	185 U	186 R	187 E	
188 C	189 T	190 Y	191 R	192 L	193 E	194 Z	195 X	196 H	197 K	
198 Y	199 Z₁	200 B	201 Z	202 N	203 C	204 L	205 F	206 B	207 T	208 H
209 X	210 O	211 J								

No. 28

CLUES

A. Chief; of the highest quality . . .

B. Supreme happiness

C. Magnum opus of Richard Harris Barham (followed by WORD D) . . .

D. See WORD C

E. Autobiographical account by Mark Twain (2 wds. after *The*)

F. Pretentious, inflated

G. Hurry

H. 1680 tragedy in blank verse by Otway (after *The*)

I. Caprice

J. Am. writer (1857–1948; "The Conqueror"; "Black Oxen")

K. Hero of "Jane Eyre"

L. Insolently bold

M. Obliterates (2 wds.)

N. Manual

O. Put out of existence

P. Historic action taken by South Carolina, Dec. 20, 1860

Q. The firmament, highest heaven

R. "Who ___ wine, woman and song, / He is a fool his whole life long" (2 wds.; Thackeray, "A Credo")

S. Gets by persistent, insidious efforts (2 wds.)

T. Eng. playwright ("Look Back in Anger"), first of the Angry Young Men

U. 1959 film starring Simone Signoret and Lawrence Harvey (4 wds.)

V. Throw a pitch dangerously close to (a batter) (2 wds.)

W. Soaks in water or other liquid

WORDS

A. 84 180 35 184 147

B. 13 5 172 36 143 116

C. 24 71 169 100 135 176 136 112 86

D. 134 32 190 70 171 90 8

E. 170 189 50 88 140 40 104 99 157 174 94 65 48 26 111

F. 16 59 46 85 137 121 98

G. 53 186 34 76 66

H. 153 129 64 2 92 97

I. 52 151 168 29 19 133 182 148 69 130 159 113

J. 110 183 78 125 49 15 156 119

K. 179 10 58 108 118 33 164 23 126

L. 4 37 47 188 83 44 106

M. 132 28 154 181 117 43 80 77

N. 3 175 177 74 158 89 105 42 163 115 27

O. 14 139 149 9 82 21 173 75 150 96

P. 165 61 114 95 25 62 18 138 187

Q. 57 146 155 45 167 109 68 81

R. 6 123 67 185 107 22 161 144

S. 87 128 31 142 39 145 7 1

T. 63 120 56 103 127 11 152

U. 17 178 101 60 54 12 73 91 51 131 141 38

V. 102 41 93 20 166 124 162

W. 122 72 160 79 30 55

Diagram (cell number — clue letter)

1 S	2 H	3 N	4 L	5 B	6 R	7 S
8 D	9 O	10 K	11 T	12 U	13 B	14 O	15 J	16 F	17 U
18 P	19 I	20 V	21 O	22 R	23 K	24 C	25 P	26 E	27 N
28 M	29 I	30 W	31 S	32 D	33 K	34 G	35 A	36 B	37 L
38 U	39 S	40 E	41 V	42 N	43 M	44 L	45 Q	46 F	47 L	48 E
49 J	50 E	51 U	52 I	53 G	54 U	55 W	56 T	57 Q
58 K	59 F	60 U	61 P	62 P	63 T	64 H	65 E	66 G	67 R
68 Q	69 I	70 D	71 C	72 W	73 U	74 N	75 O	76 G	77 M
78 J	79 W	80 M	81 Q	82 O	83 L	84 A	85 F	86 C	87 S
88 E	89 N	90 D	91 U	92 H	93 V	94 E	95 P	96 O	97 H
98 F	99 E	100 C	101 U	102 V	103 T	104 E	105 N	106 L
107 R	108 K	109 Q	110 J	111 E	112 C	113 I	114 P	115 N
116 B	117 M	118 K	119 J	120 T	121 F	122 W	123 R	124 V	125 J
126 K	127 T	128 S	129 H	130 I	131 U	132 M	133 I	134 D	135 C
136 C	137 F	138 P	139 O	140 E	141 U	142 S	143 B	144 R
145 S	146 Q	147 A	148 I	149 O	150 O	151 I	152 T	153 H
154 M	155 Q	156 J	157 E	158 N	159 I	160 W	161 R	162 V	163 N
164 K	165 P	166 V	167 Q	168 I	169 C	170 E	171 D	172 B	173 O
174 E	175 N	176 C	177 N	178 U	179 K	180 A	181 M	182 I	183 J
184 A	185 R	186 G	187 P	188 L	189 E	190 D

No. 29

CLUES

A. "First with beef and captain's ___" (Thackeray, "Little Billee"). — 187 104 226 26 73 53 8 36

B. Wilde poem beginning, "Come down, O Christ, and help me!" (2 wds.) — 225 172 101 214 80 14 5 203 135

C. Oblique shifts of rays of light. — 81 123 178 185 148 7 39 224 201 140 22

D. Landor poem beginning, "Ah, what avails the sceptred race" (2 wds.) — 153 177 156 91 213 208 206 110 15 78

E. "Number, weight, and measure in a ___" (3 wds.; Blake, "Proverbs of Hell") — 161 152 82 130 86 183 215 211 114 90 4 2

F. Mottled variety of the species Phaseolus vulgaris (2 wds.) — 159 68 151 1 171 89 30 12 17

G. River of ancient Babylon. — 196 35 158 122 125 184 189 145 100

H. Unreservedly. — 173 25 119 67 216 55 163 121

I. Actress Marisa ___ ("The Rose Tattoo"). — 138 34 29 126 49

J. Eng. literary scholar and author (1898–1963; "Out of the Silent Planet") — 200 3 117 28 85

K. Gave the validity of law; decreed. — 168 143 164 33 103 182 84

L. Deadly servings (2 wds.) — 160 139 72 63 92 210 79 132 13 47 41

M. Reconciled; granted. — 205 144 209 77 109 195 219 116

N. Stingy person. — 102 40 66 202 108 221 141

O. Wackford Squeers's school where Nicholas Nickleby gets a position (2 wds.) — 136 199 223 11 56 31 129 113 18 96 6 76 175

P. Horns called brow, bay, royal, and crown. — 75 43 218 106 137 10 169

Q. Japanese carved ornament used to fasten small objects to a sash. — 174 21 95 193 70 46 134

R. Clear, marked, well-defined. — 20 167 99 165 38 83 207 62

S. Testing, decisive. — 69 24 157 204 118 48 166

T. Singly (3 wds.) — 9 61 150 197 176 149 16

U. Combative. — 186 194 71 45 23 105 147 51

V. Lakes, pools; marshes (chiefly Brit.) — 133 98 74 97 58

W. Heedless, casual. — 42 54 88 181 222 115 93 198 170 154

X. Irritates. — 217 142 192 180 57 32 94

Y. Having the power of imaginative penetration. — 60 112 212 87 220 120 128 179 191 44

Z. "Sometime ___ of heaven shines" (4 wds.; Shakespeare, Sonnet 18). — 27 190 19 52 146 124 162 107 37 59 155 64

Z₁. State flower of New Mexico. — 50 188 127 131 65

GRID

1 F · 2 E · 3 J · 4 E · 5 B · 6 O · 7 C · 8 A · 9 T

10 P · 11 O · 12 F · 13 L · 14 B · 15 D · 16 T · 17 F · 18 O

19 Z · 20 R · 21 Q · 22 C · 23 U · 24 S · 25 H · 26 A · 27 Z · 28 J · 29 I

30 F · 31 O · 32 X · 33 K · 34 I · 35 G · 36 A · 37 Z · 38 R · 39 C

40 N · 41 L · 42 W · 43 P · 44 Y · 45 U · 46 Q · 47 L · 48 S

49 I · 50 Z₁ · 51 U · 52 Z · 53 A · 54 W · 55 H · 56 O · 57 X · 58 V · 59 Z

60 Y · 61 T · 62 R · 63 L · 64 Z · 65 Z₁ · 66 N · 67 H · 68 F

69 S · 70 Q · 71 U · 72 L · 73 A · 74 V · 75 P · 76 O · 77 M · 78 D · 79 L

80 B · 81 C · 82 E · 83 R · 84 K · 85 J · 86 E · 87 Y · 88 W

98 V · 99 R · 100 G · 101 B · 102 N · 103 K · 104 A · 105 U · 106 P · 107 Z · 108 N

109 M · 110 D · 111 T · 112 Y · 113 O · 114 E · 115 W · 116 M · 117 J · 118 S

119 H · 120 Y · 121 H · 122 G · 123 C · 124 Z · 125 G · 126 I · 127 Z₁ · 128 Y

129 O · 130 E · 131 Z₁ · 132 L · 133 V · 134 Q · 135 B · 136 O · 137 P · 138 I

139 L · 140 C · 141 N · 142 X · 143 K · 144 M · 145 G · 146 Z · 147 N · 148 C

149 T · 150 T · 151 F · 152 E · 153 D · 154 W · 155 Z · 156 D · 157 R · 158 G

159 F · 160 L · 161 E · 162 Z · 163 H · 164 K · 165 R · 166 S · 167 R · 168 K

169 P · 170 W · 171 F · 172 B · 173 H · 174 Q · 175 O · 176 T · 177 D

178 C · 179 Y · 180 X · 181 W · 182 K · 183 E · 184 G · 185 E · 186 U

187 A · 188 Z₁ · 189 G · 190 Z · 191 Y · 192 X · 193 Q · 194 U · 195 M · 196 G

197 T · 198 W · 199 O · 200 J · 201 C · 202 N · 203 B · 204 S · 205 M · 206 D · 207 R

208 D · 209 M · 210 L · 211 E · 212 Y · 213 D · 214 B · 215 E · 216 H · 217 X

218 P · 219 M · 220 Y · 221 N · 222 W · 223 O · 224 C · 225 B · 226 A

CLUES

A Material obtained by shredding unfelted rags. . . . .
174 101 56 115 183 142

B Slavery . . . .
7 27 121 49 57 76 179 93 30 173

C Swimming pool . . . .
119 95 190 192 151 172 51 18 13

D City on the Rhine, S central West Germany . . . .
28 156 43 138 146

E Viscera . . . .
137 103 194 113 145 170 34

F "Let's kill all the ____", says Dick, the Butcher ("Henry VI, Part II"). . .
164 59 108 2 40 80 91

G Brought the head of a vessel into the wind, with sails shaking . . .
11 189 36 3 111 33

H Daughter of Inachus who was transformed into a heifer. . . .
132 44

I Feeling of dread . . . .
144 60 104 83 186

J Position of something surrounded by other things . . . . .
58 79 12 167 135

K Expressed in words . . . . . .
191 78 39 64 134 71 120

L Wickerwork material . . . . . .
94 46 77 100 26 161

M "Thrice as blind as any noon-tide ____" (Tennyson, "The Holy Grail") . . . .
117 70 153

N Yellow . . . .

O Fairy queen . . . .
85 160 141 128 68 17 152 177

P "Spring goeth all ____" (2 wds.; Bridges, "Spring") . . . . .
25 87 16

Q Fiber used for matting, baskets, hats, etc. . . . .
178 96 23 29 140 48 149

R Harmonious motion or proportion
133 168 55 125 102 181

S Harbach-Kern song from "Roberta" . . . .
38 118 50 129 88 107 148 45 61

T All wet, wide of the mark (2 wds.)
180 130 163 19 14 112 86 32 62 147

U Loose. . . . .
99 42 89 105 123 66 22

V Thick-set. . . . .
106 182 116 176 54 5 63 75

W Wearing down . . . .
150 31 35 114 97 82

X "'Tho' faith and form / Be sunder'd in the ____" (3 wds.; Tennyson, "In Memoriam") . . . .
90 110 73 127 185 136 193 10 169

Y Prop temporarily supporting a pole or mast being erected 2 wds.).
21 53 166 122 81 188 37 131 69 171 65

Z Hustling, busy (3 wds.) . . . .
154 165 4 162 155 109 98

Z₁ Eng. writer (1904-1986; "Prater Violet") . . . .
24 72 52 187 143 1 74 157 139

Z₂ Menace; warning . . . .
9 6 47 175 15 124

CLUES   WORDS

A Advantage gained for some purpose. 135 187 14 33 198 157 147 78

B N Am. labiate herb having showy bright-red flowers (2 wds.). . .   81 26 149 74 51 168 120 100 57

C "Branched thoughts, new grown with pleasant pain, / Instead of pines shall murmur ___" (3 wds.; Keats, "Ode to Psyche"). . .   105 95 189 148 44 79 112 7 185

D Shuts out, clobbers 165 123 35 48 83 88

E Serving to distinguish. 128 190 181 11 20 172 41 85 24 116 109

F Tympanic membranes 196 91 117 132 82 67 45 34

G Gutbucket 36 63 71 171 93 143 6 25 108 87

H Unwilling, loath 47 186 18 10 102 96

I Great New Orleans jazz cornetist (1885–1938; full name) 99 56 162 66 127 54 118 43 90 104

J Exclamatory sentence or striking reflection which concludes a passage. 72 125 146 115 89 160 156 175 86 39

K Aspires; feels strong tenderness .   151 164 166 126 13 37

L Formal expressions of high praise. 60 159 201 136 179 42 152

M Oral; designative (of a will) 158 107 200 73 129 180 97 84 22 32 9

N Flagrant 137 59 192 183 62 50 174

O Milan's opera house (2 wds.). . . .   114 197 124 191 134 167 70

P Complexities. 49 40 142 188 133 163 176 194 182 131 17

Q Toffs, dandies 27 169 15 195 113 177

R Deuterium oxide (2 wds.). 145 46 199 55 110 111 31 76 139 16

S Contends vigorously 38 138 69 23 122 2 153

T Round or oval window (hyph.) . .   65 184 94 5 101 144 170 106 29 161 52

U Hangs loosely 173 121 141 155 64 103 119

V "Within ___ of that high hall / Sate Brunswick's fated chieftain" (3 wds.; Byron, "Childe Harold").   150 28 178 77 92 140 1 21 3 154 130 30 68

W Dandies, blades, gallants, perhaps collegiate (2 wds.). 80 12 53 75 8 58 193 19 61 98

1	V	2	S			3	V	4	W		
11	E	12	W	13	V	14	A	15	Q	16	R	17	P	18	H			19	W	20	E
21	V	22	M	23	S	24	E	25	G	26	B	27	Q			28	V	29	T
30	V	31	R	32	V	33	A			34	F	35	D	36	G	37	K	38	K	39	J	40	P
41	E	42	L	43	I	44	C			45	F	46	R	47	H	48	D	49	P	50	N	51	B
52	T	53	T	54	I	55	R			56	I	57	B	58	W	59	N	60	L	61	W
62	N	63	G	64	U	65	T	66	I	67	F	68	V	69	S	70	O	71	G
72	J	73	M	74	B	75	W	76	R	77	V	78	A	79	C	80	W	81	B
82	F	83	D	84	M	85	E	86	J	87	G	88	D	89	J	90	I	91	F
92	V	93	G	94	T	95	C	96	H	97	M	98	I	99	I	100	B	101	T
102	H	103	U	104	I	105	C	106	T	107	M	108	G	109	E	110	R	111	R	112	C
113	Q	114	O	115	J	116	E	117	F	118	I	119	U	120	B	121	U	122	S
123	D	124	O	125	J	126	K	127	I	128	E	129	M	130	V	131	P	132	F
133	P	134	O	135	A	136	L	137	N	138	S	139	R	140	V	141	U	142	P
143	G	144	T	145	R	146	J	147	A	148	C	149	B	150	V	151	K	152	L
153	S	154	V	155	U	156	J	157	A	158	M	159	L	160	J	161	T	162	I
163	P	164	K	165	D	166	K	167	O	168	B	169	Q	170	T	171	G
172	E	173	U	174	N	175	J	176	P	177	Q	178	V	179	L	180	M	181	E
182	P	183	N	184	T	185	C	186	H	187	A	188	P	189	C	190	E	191	O	192	N
193	W	194	P	195	Q	196	F	197	O	198	A	199	R	200	G	201	L	202	G

No. 32

CLUES

A — Am. mystery writer (1888–1959; "Farewell, My Lovely"; full name)   `83 38 31 49 101 106 78 217 112 146 189 34 120 185 44`

B — Silk-and-wool material used in upholstery   `100 18 138 25 203 212`

C — Recreation; pastime   `15 186 116 158 73 114 96 166 134`

D — Declaim bombastically   `163 152 109 71`

E — Gloomy, sorrowful   `28 68 133 11 171 57`

F — Dippy, daffy; full of filberts, perhaps   `216 179 118 174 19`

G — Rub out; wear away   `126 184 65 35 53 3`

H — Remorse, pity   `209 56 194 175`

I — State in S India; light cotton fabric   `81 188 173 132 144 155`

J — "But I was ——, and now am full of tears" (3 wds.; Yeats, "Down by the Salley Gardens")   `60 48 169 211 87 183 200 37 39 196 92 99 204 70 128`

K — Uncommon (4 wds.)   `66 208 23 137 130 91 192 119 168 123 36 88 104 140 182 80`

L — Eng. poet (1858–1936; "World-Strangeness")   `136 54 161 13 207 93`

M — 25,661-ft. Himalayan peak (2 wds.)   `33 215 172 45 162 205 187 51 85`

N — "The Big —— I can do myself like any now going" (hyph. and wd.; Scott, "Journal 14 Mar. 1826")   `55 10 7 1 107 41 190 75 214 150 103 27`

O — Grieve inconsolably (4 wds.)   `12 6 135 52 86 129 46 95 176 113 77 170 98 90 47`

P — 1899 Henry James novel (2 wds. after *The*)   `148 42 115 111 124 59 5 26 167 218`

Q — Rash, heedless   `108 141 17 58 149 72`

R — Coloring delicately   `94 165 84 127 154 69 21`

S — Character assumed by Thackeray as literary critic and observer of manners   `50 40 121 16 43 102 202 61 213 110 143`

T — Fuddy-duddy; strait-laced   `20 29 24 97 125 195`

U — Small case for needles, toilet articles, etc.   `64 201 197 131`

V — Disaster   `147 79 145 32 160 191 67 178 89 2 22`

W — Destroying   `30 157 210 153 62 177 122`

X — "Since —— became a gentleman" (2 wds. "Richard III")   `139 151 76 117 206 156 198 9 63`

Y — Kind of knotted lace   `164 193 142 159 199 4 181`

Z — Employ, hire; bind oneself to work, as by putting one's name to paper (2 wds.)   `74 14 105 8 82 180`

No. 33

CLUES

A Oddball, character, codger. . . . . .

B Make pure; clarify. . . . .

C Reserved, cool, aloof. . . . .

D 9th-cen. Eng. prelate, saint whose day is July 15 . . . .

E Used up . . . .

F "The Aristocrat who cleans ____" (2 wds.; Gilbert, "The Gondoliers") . .

G Intrudes, meddles (2 wds.). . . . . .

H Glorification; raising to high rank. . .

I Titaness, daughter of Uranus and Gaea . . . .

J Changes, exchanges; gets along . . . .

K Tall, trumpet-shaped drinking glass with a bulb at the closed end (hyph.)

L "Not a flower sweet, / On my black ____ let there be strown" ("Twelfth Night") . . . .

M Joan of Arc and Portia, e.g. . . . . .

N Instrument for measuring electrical resistance. . . . .

O Most elevated or sublime. . . . . . .

P Differently. . . . .

Q Deteriorates, conks out; dries up (3 wds.) . . . .

R Occurrences, minor episodes. . . . . .

S Participate; contribute; pay (2 wds.) .

T Connie Mack's ball club, 1901–50 . .

U Hawaiian island west of Maui and type of veranda named for it . . . .

V Does wrong . . . .

W Singly (4 wds.) . . . .

X Lambastes; gives what-for (2 wds.) . .

Y Paris green, e.g. . . . .

Z "Here's to the flaunting, ____ ; / And here's to the housewife that's thrifty" (2 wds.; Sheridan, "School for Scandal") . . . .

Z₁ "I never get between ____ / But I smell Sussex air" (2 wds.; Belloc, "The South Country") . . . .

Z₂ "A violet in the ____" (4 wds., "Hamlet") . . . .

WORDS

A 197 47 97 139 121 224

B 99 223 94 37 187 8

C 1 103 28 138 216 199

D 45 42 182 12 96 32 129

E 79 173 208 49 62

F 151 213 184 189 93 218 175 205

G 153 51 55 183 172 134 229

H 107 180 226 27 46 22 128 169 75 68 135

I 203 30 71 164 106 125

J 83 120 215 181 89 18

K 39 148 78 141 168 142 228 177 17

L 65 179 166 5 150 2

M 7 163 167 143 123 221 48 147

N 193 210 185 124 59 118 66 162

O 40 204 20 50 64 54 156 61

P 171 95 127 52 192 63 155 113 77

Q 110 131 186 34 6 220 202 4 29

R 67 112 56 82 92 140 160 209 26

S 16 74 108 133 60 149

T 69 207 43 137 91 122 174 178 24

U 219 136 146 117 100 11

V 58 206 36 227

W 104 196 102 35 90 44 198 145 9 31

X 98 158 116 72 19 10 87 119

Y 195 81 132 154 15 73 111 85 225 165 214

Z 25 53 126 144 176 194 114 222 211 33 157 86 21 200 41 217

Z₁ 212 130 3 76 88 109 159 13

Z₂ 152 201 14 188 170 80 161 191 70 57 101 190 115 84 38 23 105 230

No. 34

CLUES

WORDS

A Small, fresh-water relative of the lobster . . . .
108 64 197 91 142 96 42 186

B Languid . . . .
159 5 199 189 48 58 176 29

C London arena . . . .
60 79 185 88 37 17 4 104 126 44 114 175

D Sister-wife and brother-husband of anc. Egypt (3 wds.) . . . .
101 111 149 221 77 25 209 143 31 2 40 27 155

E Overwhelm, crush (2 wds.) . .
70 113 63 90 179 115 124

F Preoccupy greatly . . . .
196 177 137 110 87 223

G Fends off . . . .
207 53 174 86 220 23 130

H "What this country needs is a good five-cent ___" (Franklin P. Adams) . . . . .
85 123 20 180 153 158

I Called for; made necessary . .
164 51 21 170 67 216 76

J Mink's relative . . . .
212 66 140 147 13

K Sustained . . . .
206 52 59 9 152 201

L Champagne center . . . .
195 163 134 56 128 117

M Beclouds . . . .
148 107 62 198 139 50 173

N Furniture, equipment . . . . .
172 166 35 129 200 61 103 122 46 133 3 55

O Revive . . . .
100 41 210 19 32 98 45

P "Oft the ear the open ___ tire" (Pope, "Essay on Criticism") . . . .
57 178 156 222 94 190

Q Inordinate . . . .
195 163 134 56 128 117

R Saves (2 wds.) . . . .
188 22 109 119 138 38 65 83 219

S Doctor who emphasizes the musculo-skeletal system . . .
127 132 141 112 191 1 75 14

T "Merrily, merrily shall I live now / ___ that hangs on the bough" (3 wds., "The Tempest") . . . .
34 69 193 136 218 33 36 18 118 78 71 181 161 47 184

U Raised framework . . . .
43 8 7 16 26 205 171 105

V Outdid . . . .
214 80 39 167 157 151

W Combines harmoniously . . .
24 169 120 146 89 203 30 144 183 97 208 81

X So close as to leave the outcome in doubt (3 wds.) . .
54 93 204 116 6 49 11 165 135 73

Y Chatter . . . .
125 160 194

Z Advantage (2 wds.) . . . . . .
12 182 217 95 211 74 15 192 150

Z₁ Captivation: Var. sp. . . . . .
68 10 82 92 28 154 187 213 202 102 131

No. 35

CLUES

	Clue	WORDS
A	Destroy utterly	24 185 38 175 12 80 144 112 91 42
B	Capital (2 wds.)	118 68 127 153 133 195 32 59 216
C	Trains, instructs	215 56 84 72 184 41 3
D	In addition (2 wds.)	190 132 138 186 37 53
E	The act of drinking	96 1 54 46 193 150 187 191 164 220
F	Followed by WORD V: 1931 novel by Saint-Exupéry	168 121 221 62 39
G	Broadcasting by wireless	160 171 183 104 143 107 119 188
H	Inspiring reverential wonder or dread	57 75 159 149 105 170 212
I	Roundworm or threadworm	48 123 101 173 16 111 169 74
J	Traffic; bargain	27 60 49 18 117 92 204 146 189
K	Increase rapidly	177 108 148 115 95 167 103 202
L	Sharp, quick cries	203 125 89 67 198
M	1925 Pulitzer Prize-winning play by George Kelly (2 wds.)	23 110 66 90 82 155 130 145 28 199
N	Thrashing	180 44 136 22 152 14
O	Inquest, the writ instituting it, or the verdict	196 45 166 34 174 206
P	Remarkable, outstanding	86 163 200 194 154 2 100 51 79 182
Q	J. F. Cooper hero (2 wds.)	70 135 61 179 214 109 58 31 158 8 126
R	Slip away	15 161 208 137 5 50
S	Werewolf	128 64 78 207 106 141 65 30 13 142 40
T	Far eastern transport longed for in a 1948 song (2 wds.)	178 120 99 83 73 7 94 209
U	Stubborn	35 17 147 97 210 88 176 157 77 219 43 134
V	See WORD F	98 9 20 172 201 33
W	Tight spot	124 26 114 165 25 181
X	1822 song by G. Kiallmark and Samuel Woodworth (3 wds., after *The*)	29 213 113 47 102 218 129 81 162 140 93 122 85 21
Y	Puppies	11 131 63 19 87 116
Z	Result	55 211 10 36 192 197 76 223 69
Z₁	Copy; rehearsal	205 217 156 6 4 52 71 222 139 151

Grid

7 T	8 Q	9 V	10 Z	▓	1 E	2 P	3 C	4 Z₁	▓	5 R	6 Z₁
17 U	18 J	19 Y	20 V	21 X	22 N	23 M	▓	11 Y	12 A	13 S	14 N	15 R	16 I
27 J	28 M	29 X	30 S	31 Q	32 B	33 V	34 O	35 U	36 Z	37 D
38 A	39 F	40 S	▓	41 C	42 A	43 U	44 N	45 O	46 E	47 X	48 I
49 J	50 R	51 P	52 Z₁	53 D	54 E	55 Z	56 C	57 H
58 Q	59 B	60 J	61 Q	62 F	63 Y	64 S	65 S	66 M	67 L
68 B	69 Z	70 Q	71 Z₁	72 C	73 T	74 I	75 H	76 Z
77 U	78 S	79 P	80 A	81 X	82 M	83 T	84 C	85 X	86 P
87 Y	88 U	89 L	90 M	91 A	92 J	93 X	94 T	95 K	96 E	97 U
98 V	99 T	100 P	101 I	102 X	103 K	104 G	105 H	106 S	107 G	108 K
109 Q	110 M	111 I	112 A	113 X	114 W	115 K	116 Y	117 J	118 B
119 G	120 T	121 F	122 X	123 I	124 W	125 L	126 Q	127 B	128 S	129 X
130 M	131 Y	132 D	133 B	134 U	135 Q	136 N	137 R	138 D
139 Z₁	140 X	141 S	142 S	143 G	144 A	145 M	146 J	147 U	148 K	149 H
150 E	151 Z₁	152 N	153 B	154 P	155 M	156 Z₁	157 U	158 Q	159 H
160 G	161 R	162 X	163 P	164 E	165 W	166 O	167 K	168 F	169 I
170 H	171 G	172 V	173 I	174 O	175 A	176 U	177 K	178 T	179 Q
180 N	181 W	182 P	183 G	184 C	185 A	186 D	187 E	188 G
189 J	190 D	191 E	192 Z	193 E	194 P	195 B	196 O	197 Z	198 L
199 M	200 P	201 V	202 K	203 L	204 J	205 Z₁	206 O	207 S
208 R	209 T	210 U	211 Z	212 H	213 X	214 Q	215 C	216 B	217 Z₁	218 X
219 U	220 E	221 F	222 Z₁	223 Z

No. 36

CLUES

	Clue	Word numbers
A	Eng. merchant, founder of the YMCA; knighted in 1894 (full name).	178 166 158 187 79 46 31 85 100 52 16 109 170 145
B	Obstinate.	149 119 191 4 108 161
C	Heed.	107 42 98 78 177 88 113 70 91
D	Jacob's favorite wife (Gen. 29-35).	84 141 189 151 198 53
E	Bantu language of Cape Province, South Africa.	63 182 104 138 80
F	Up against it, in for it (3 wds.).	93 29 20 49 181 143 38 7 86 129
G	Traditional name of a Rembrandt painting until it was cleaned in the 1940's, revealing the name to be wrong (2 wds.).	41 176 30 18 150 106 193 160 133 59
H	Sudden, sharp pain.	105 54 126 26 6 11
I	Sated.	33 68 12 122 40 197 114
J	Manifest.	48 179 69 28 8 13 115
K	Subdues.	43 173 50 137 94
L	Suspicion of injury; offense.	180 165 96 112 25 128 186
M	Outlay.	23 136 22 58
N	Egyptian god of wisdom, learning, and magic.	125 55 116 47 140
O	Gilbert & Sullivan fairy.	5 142 175 132
P	Equip.	89 97 17 117 74 139
Q	Polaris (2 wds.).	155 148 67 83 196 110 19 99 157
R	Beliefs, positions.	95 130 57 62 1 184
S	Guacharo.	44 121 66 77 135 2 87
T	Habit.	15 164 45 185
U	Am. novelist (1843-1916; "The Aspern Papers"; full name).	24 154 172 199 183 131 169 120 162 61
V	Fresh.	3 32 194 73 118 156 64 92
W	Mitigate.	190 71 34 90 39 123 65 174 152
X	Small deposits of water.	35 111 163
Y	Callous.	72 127 146 10 60 192 102 167 103
Z	Delightful; fascinating.	168 37 144 147 153 21 81 195
Z₁	Metronomic function (2 wds.).	9 51 56 14 36 76 27 134 82 159 171

No. 37

CLUES

		WORDS
A	Mayor of New York who resigned under a cloud of scandal in 1932	94 196 145 172 54 151 128 71 166 141 208
B	Henry James novel (2 wds. after *The*)	37 199 22 168 142 65 192 156 184 95
C	Intone	81 2 187 191 98
D	Feathered serpent god of the Aztecs and Toltecs	48 33 14 137 32 200 154 96 135 62 44 67
E	Escort	143 148 99 47 78
F	External parasite	70 101 110 183 17 116 90
G	Pretended, false	15 84 159 195
H	Encounter	209 202 134 73 59 206
I	Plant of the caraway genus, used as a medicine and as a condiment	57 158 74 127 190 10
J	Payments to authors, composers, etc.	186 55 201 164 177 203 170 5 43
K	Animal-lover	31 13 27 34 113 155 51 68 39 36
L	Arbitrary decree	92 69 133 111 64
M	Irritated	150 61 53 18 153 161 23
N	Slaughterhouse	6 132 80 160 93 188 42 211
O	About to happen (2 wds.)	181 120 162 212 107 140 194
P	"Unfading ——, immortal flies" (Brooke, "Heaven")	41 24 182 205 130
Q	Baseball trophy, for instance	77 89 171 26 114 108 7
R	Vientiane is its capital	58 20 176 91
S	Stroking movement in massage	144 180 117 118 178 49 28 103 86 3
T	Transversely	50 112 45 25 125 147 83
U	Wee drams	16 119 76 38
V	Incoherent	174 207 66 29 139 35 124 167 100 12
W	Unsteady; feeble; loony	63 9 131 1 179
X	Way of thinking; metaphysics	87 189 85 149 123 175 198 129
Y	Cycle	173 109 88 79 126 40 115 52 122 105
Z	Am. musical comedy star (1909–84; full name)	185 106 138 210 21 157 46 60 163 30 197
Z_1	Genus of tropical Am. orchids	121 75 204 19 102 11 72 169
Z_2	Abner smote Asahel "under ——," that the spear came out behind him" (3 wds., II Sam. 2:23)	8 193 146 56 152 136 97 82 165 104 4

No. 38

CLUES

A. 1961 Tennessee Williams play (4 wds.)
B. 1952 Hemingway novella (5 wds. after *The*)
C. Outdoors
D. Limp
E. Unsubstantial or haphazardly contrived (hyph.)
F. General idea or term; theory; visionary notion
G. English primrose having yellow flowers
H. Flower related to WORD G
I. Card game played by a banker and punters who bet against him
J. Faucet or peg for stopping the flow of liquid
K. Cap. of Alpes Maritimes, France
L. Favorable reception; the act of assenting or believing
M. Error or slip in conduct
N. Sturdy fabric used in men's clothing (2 wds.)
O. 1942 film with Bette Davis and Paul Henreid (2 wds.)
P. Conjectures, surmises
Q. Taunts, flouts, mocks
R. Honor, laudatory notice
S. 1950 Kirk Douglas film (5 wds.)
T. 1851 play by Eugene M. Labiche (3 wds. after *The*)
U. One who bestows favors on relatives
V. Am. critic and author (1895–1972; "Patriotic Gore"; full name)
W. IDs for GIs (2 wds.)
X. Anc. Gr. youths just entering manhood
Y. Bigoted, intolerant (hyph.)

WORDS

Clue	Cells
A	59 44 13 187 126 65 227 210 138 104 201 169 89 221 100 116
B	107 199 219 95 125 15 214 3 78 204 176 62 111 188 71
C	147 198 160 105 4 21 93 110
D	179 47 129 91 226 149
E	130 12 181 156 92 115 87 136 225 60
F	209 196 1 200 17 157 144 24 171 88 57
G	137 31 230 83 146 99 103
H	7 215 143 46 28
I	180 27 158 132 58 193 67 151
J	49 220 33 185 229 109
K	42 74 86 53
L	97 141 8 114 61 159 218 82 192 118
M	124 165 140 175 155 20 96
N	168 161 22 166 9 148 35 14 79 153
O	38 94 183 43 112 173 197 56 184 63
P	186 55 10 106 117 217 75
Q	150 213 98 123 6 154 34
R	77 80 5 182 228 174 11 127
S	2 81 48 222 178 163 224 108 134 119 36 206 164 25 52 40
T	41 172 121 212 177 189 30 64 133 232 39 195 135 102 69
U	170 37 54 128 19 29 191 211
V	194 45 76 145 122 216 205 85 68 32 152 23
W	167 50 101 26 18 202 90
X	231 84 203 131 208 72
Y	120 142 70 51 162 223 113 139 66 207 16 190

Grid

1 F	2 S	3 B	4 C	5 R	6 Q	7 H	8 L	9 N

- Row: 10 P · 11 R · 12 E · 13 A · 14 N · 15 B · 16 Y · 17 F · 18 W · 19 U · 20 M
- Row: 21 C · 22 N · 23 V · 24 F · 25 S · 26 W · 27 I · 28 H · 29 U · 30 T
- Row: 31 G · 32 V · 33 J · 34 Q · 35 N · 36 S · 37 U · 38 O · 39 T · 40 S
- Row: 41 T · 42 K · 43 O · 44 A · 45 V · 46 H · 47 D · 48 S · 49 J · 50 W
- Row: 51 Y · 52 S · 53 K · 54 U · 55 P · 56 O · 57 F · 58 L · 59 A · 60 E
- Row: 61 L · 62 B · 63 O · 64 T · 65 A · 66 Y · 67 I · 68 V · 69 T · 70 Y · 71 B
- Row: 72 X · 73 S · 74 K · 75 P · 76 V · 77 R · 78 B · 79 N · 80 R
- Row: 81 S · 82 L · 83 G · 84 X · 85 V · 86 K · 87 E · 88 F · 89 A · 90 W · 91 D
- Row: 92 E · 93 C · 94 O · 95 B · 96 M · 97 L · 98 Q · 99 G · 100 A · 101 W
- Row: 102 T · 103 G · 104 A · 105 C · 106 P · 107 B · 108 S · 109 J · 110 C
- Row: 111 B · 112 O · 113 Y · 114 L · 115 E · 116 A · 117 P · 118 L · 119 S · 120 Y
- Row: 121 T · 122 V · 123 Q · 124 M · 125 B · 126 A · 127 R · 128 U · 129 D · 130 E · 131 X
- Row: 132 I · 133 T · 134 S · 135 T · 136 E · 137 G · 138 A · 139 Y · 140 M
- Row: 141 L · 142 Y · 143 H · 144 F · 145 V · 146 G · 147 C · 148 N · 149 D · 150 Q · 151 I
- Row: 152 V · 153 N · 154 Q · 155 M · 156 E · 157 F · 158 I · 159 L · 160 C · 161 N
- Row: 162 Y · 163 S · 164 S · 165 M · 166 N · 167 W · 168 N · 169 A · 170 U · 171 F
- Row: 172 T · 173 O · 174 R · 175 M · 176 B · 177 T · 178 S · 179 D · 180 I · 181 E
- Row: 182 R · 183 O · 184 O · 185 J · 186 P · 187 A · 188 B · 189 T · 190 Y · 191 U
- Row: 192 L · 193 I · 194 V · 195 T · 196 F · 197 O · 198 C · 199 B · 200 F · 201 A · 202 W
- Row: 203 X · 204 B · 205 V · 206 V · 207 Y · 208 X · 209 F · 210 A · 211 U · 212 T · 213 Q
- Row: 214 B · 215 H · 216 V · 217 P · 218 L · 219 B · 220 J · 221 A · 222 S · 223 Y
- Row: 224 S · 225 E · 226 D · 227 A · 228 J · 229 J · 230 G · 231 X · 232 T

No. 39

CLUES

WORDS

A. Wander about, gazing vacantly — 120 160 42 65

B. First-magnitude star of the constellation Taurus — 13 168 7 187 179 110 49 137 161

C. First-rate; A number 1 — 85 157 90 51 28 191

D. Minute black insect, common in flowers — 38 148 181 107 121 150

E. Sanctity — 136 171 22 53 32 125 71 82

F. Science of bettering humans through improved environment — 145 84 156 68 57 135

G. Cricket bat — 50 75 72 173 37 103 20 186 142

H. Pertinent; with reference or regard to — 126 112 31 87 139 2 60

I. Voraciousness — 153 24 48 5 104 167 61 40

J. Passage from upper to lower New York Bay (after *The*) — 44 140 94 58 36 83 131

K. Just in case; given the remote possibility (4 wds.) — 192 14 41 166 46 9 151 56 100 86 185 80 118 4

L. Hits high in the air — 177 67 134 33 76

M. Extract by evaporation and condensation (Br. sp.) — 164 43 144 124 16 108

N. Hindu woman's garment — 141 114 98 159

O. Type of portable shelter — 147 102 117 27

P. *Crème de la crème*, "400" (2 wds.) — 30 35 111 180 10 63 3 149 99 93

Q. Reward or punishment that is merited — 18 123 170 26 195 89

R. First commercially successful comic strip character, created by R.F. Outcault (2 wds. after *The*) — 196 155 52 109 152 19 15 176 128

S. Chance; propitious occasion — 34 172 183 62 39 194 97 163 79 138 95

T. Stronghold; in N America, a trading post — 54 119 47 132

U. Sententious, moralizing character in "Hamlet" — 165 130 184 96 127 146 81 74

V. Exceed in importance — 64 70 29 175 55 116 158 23

W. Products or profits of land which has been sown or planted — 182 129 189 178 193 1 11 6 77 66

X. Beginner (Var.) — 45 101 115 169

Y. Regeneration; fresh beginning — 154 92 17 143 106 78 122

Z. 1913 song sung by Judy Garland to a photo of Clark Gable in "Broadway Melody of 1938" (5 wds.) — 190 71 88 12 162 188 69 8 105 21 73 25 113 174 133 59

Grid

1 W	2 H	3 P	4 K	5 I	6 W	7 B	8 Z	9 K	10 P
11 W	12 Z	13 B	14 K	15 R	16 M	17 Y	18 Q	19 R	20 F
21 Z	22 E	23 V	24 I	25 Z	26 Q	27 O	28 C	29 V	
30 P	31 H	32 E	33 L	34 S	35 P	36 J	37 G	38 D	39 S
40 I	41 K	42 A	43 M	44 J	45 X	46 K	47 T	48 I	49 B
50 F	51 C	52 R	53 E	54 T	55 V	56 K	57 F	58 J	
59 Z	60 H	61 I	62 S	63 P	64 V	65 A	66 W	67 L	68 F
69 Z	70 V	71 E	72 G	73 Z	74 U	75 G	76 L	77 W	
78 Y	79 S	80 K	81 U	82 E	83 J	84 G	85 C	86 K	87 H
88 Z	89 Q	90 C	91 Z	92 Y	93 P	94 J	95 S	96 U	97 S
98 N	99 P	100 K	101 X	102 O	103 G	104 I	105 D	106 Y	107 D
108 M	109 R	110 B	111 P	112 H	113 Z	114 N	115 X	116 V	117 O
118 K	119 T	120 A	121 D	122 Y	123 Q	124 M	125 E	126 H	127 U
129 W	130 U	131 J	132 T	133 Z	134 L	135 G	136 E	137 B	
138 S	139 H	140 J	141 N	142 F	143 Y	144 M	145 G	146 U	147 O
148 D	149 P	150 D	151 K	152 R	153 I	154 Y	155 R	156 G	
157 C	158 V	159 N	160 A	161 B	162 Z	163 S	164 M	165 U	166 K
167 I	168 B	169 X	170 Q	171 E	172 S	173 G	174 Z	175 V	176 R
177 L	178 W	179 B	180 P	181 D	182 W	183 S	184 U	185 K	186 G
188 Z	189 W	190 Z	191 C	192 K	193 W	194 S	195 Q	196 R	

No. 40

CLUES

A Very intelligent or talented · · · 159 9 164 56 5 140

B Grants; acknowledges · · · · · · · · 82 186 37 76 179 144

C Hubbub, rumpus · · · · · · · · · 69 42 66 30 89 38 107 119

D Mete, distribute (2 wds.) · · · · · · 174 7 27 72 131 155 48

E Whiffets, jackstraws · · · · · · · · 133 70 75 121 8 172 198 150

F Philosophical work by Søren
   Kierkegaard (2 wds.) · · · · · · 16 175 134 141 113 192 65 45

G 1872 Mark Twain book (2 wds.) · · 64 13 132 11 81 3 110 154 90 157

H Is prominent (2 wds.) · · · · · · · · 74 52 21 91 127 143 152 36 161

I Wine pitcher of Greek and
   Roman antiquity · · · · · · · · · · 138 142 26 170 19 2 126 149

J Of no consequence · · · · · · · · · 85 33 73 101 22 106 63 125 194 51 135

K Those who are not of a certain
   profession · · · · · · · · · · · · · · 197 18 128 104 61

L Intercalation, as of a day in a
   year · · · · · · · · · · · · · · · · · 50 112 193 46 23 145 15 130

M Ger. novelist and essayist
   (1875-1965; "Buddenbrooks") · · · 105 12 35 71 123 67 97 109 173 10

N A leading character in Tom
   Taylor's play, "The Ticket-of-
   Leave Man" · · · · · · · · · · · · 151 87 78 20 178 122 96 77

O Former · · · · · · · · · · · · · · · · 102 59 129 80 1 93 115 148 167

P Type of locker · · · · · · · · · · · · 4 117 43 34 120 108 187 53

Q Am. playwright and librettist
   (1873-1963; "Madame Sherry",
   "Roberta"; full name) · · · · · · 136 185 196 158 40 32 6 17 62 116 169

R 1924 musical comedy on which
   WORD Q collaborated (3 wds.) · · 29 41 156 55 166 111 181 94 153 184 160

S Main or essential part of a
   matter · · · · · · · · · · · · · · · · 147 25 95 60

T Pluck; jerk · · · · · · · · · · · · · · 92 49 103 54 88 57

U Trash · · · · · · · · · · · · · · · · · 86 100 44 68 114 183 163 189

V Vile, detestable actions · · · · · · · 188 182 165 47 28 118 139 195 79 180 177 39

W 1905 song made famous by Eva
   Tanguay (3 wds.) · · · · · · · · · 58 124 162 146 171 84 24 14 191

X Structures composed of crossed
   wooden or metal strips · · · · · · 137 176 190 99 31 83 98 168

WORDS (grid)

1 O	2 I	3 G	4 P	5 A	6 Q
7 D	8 E	9 A	10 M	11 G	12 M	13 G	14 W	15 L	16 F	17 Q
18 K	19 I	20 N	21 H	22 J	23 L	24 W	25 S	26 I	27 D
28 V	29 R	30 C	31 X	32 Q	33 J	34 P	35 M	36 H	37 B
38 C	39 V	40 Q	41 R	42 C	43 P	44 U	45 F	46 L	47 V
48 D	49 T	50 L	51 J	52 H	53 P	54 T	55 R	56 A
57 T	58 W	59 O	60 S	61 K	62 Q	63 J	64 G	65 F	66 C	67 M
68 U	69 C	70 E	71 M	72 D	73 J	74 H	75 E	76 B
77 N	78 N	79 V	80 O	81 G	82 B	83 X	84 W	85 J	86 U
87 N	88 T	89 C	90 G	91 H	92 T	93 O	94 R	95 S
96 X	97 M	98 X	99 X	100 U	101 J	102 O	103 T	104 K
105 M	106 J	107 C	108 P	109 M	110 G	111 R	112 L	113 F	114 U
115 O	116 Q	117 P	118 V	119 C	120 P	121 E	122 N	123 M	124 W
125 J	126 I	127 H	128 K	129 O	130 L	131 D	132 G	133 E	134 F
135 J	136 Q	137 X	138 I	139 V	140 A	141 F	142 I	143 H
144 B	145 L	146 W	147 S	148 O	149 I	150 E	151 N	152 H	153 R
154 G	155 D	156 R	157 G	158 Q	159 A	160 R	161 H	162 W
163 U	164 A	165 V	166 R	167 O	168 X	169 Q	170 I	171 W
172 E	173 M	174 D	175 F	176 X	177 V	178 N	179 B	180 V	181 R
182 V	183 U	184 R	185 Q	186 B	187 P	188 V	189 U	190 X	191 W	192 F
193 L	194 J	195 V	196 Q	197 K	198 E

CLUES / WORDS

A. Reciprocity 85 20 65 70 199 207 168 73 41

B. Fine fig; neatness (hyph. and wd.) 177 29 125 206 67 100 151 79 63 135 196 139 172

C. Necessity 110 14 215 160 61 34 80 147 19

D. Plains Indian of the southwest 115 201 52 208 155

E. Play by Thomas Dekker (3 wds.) 33 148 211 131 11 169 181 54 38 174 2 25 164 209

F. Sorcery 165 192 220 159 120 146 97 60 195 107

G. Credit 77 24 81 190 162 105 216 228 28

H. Annoyingly protracted 218 198 212 75 8 78 91 152 47 35 161 132

I. Eng. satirist (1567-1601); "The Unfortunate Traveler" 128 191 15 103 109

J. Shunned 3 101 214 74 9 180 45 62

K. Decoy 4 171 44 184

L. Wrap up closely 43 32 94 118 5 187 226 113

M. Indefinitely long duration 157 124 51 95 40 72 89 149 119 140

N. May of life, salad days (3 wds.) 138 96 197 193 163 114 7 58 167 117 53 225 154

O. 1937 Leo McCarey comedy with Cary Grant and Irene Dunne (2 wds. after *The*) 57 223 64 50 123 37 18 93 102 6

P. More modern 175 142 42 17 59

Q. English explorer (1593?-1635?), seeker of the Northwest Passage, author of "Strange and Dangerous Voyage" (full name) 156 112 186 200 127 13 69 99 68 158 76

R. Dusky 143 16 217 183 111 66 56

S. Haughty, contemptuous (4 wds.) 92 116 134 185 203 71 98 205 210 10 39 173 141 178 22

T. Figuratively, British journalism (2 wds.) 189 27 84 106 153 21 204 46 104 121 1

U. Forerunner of the guitar 55 36 108 86

V. Severe trial (2 wds.) 182 176 224 222 49 145 82 129

W. Goddess represented with six arms and three heads 30 221 88 166 137 122

X. Unreserved, candid, frank (hyph.) 194 144 26 219 126 83 188 12 130 179 23

Y. Motorist's aid (2 wds.) 90 170 213 87 133 31 48

Z. Give vent to 136 150 227 202

Grid

1 T	2 E	■	4 K	5 L	6 O	7 N				
8 H	9 J	10 S	11 E	12 X	13 Q	14 C	15 I	16 R	17 P	
18 O	19 C	20 A	21 T	22 S	23 X	24 G	25 E	26 X		
27 T	28 G	29 B	30 W	31 Y	32 L	33 E	34 C	35 H	36 U	37 O
38 E	39 S	40 M	41 A	42 P	43 L	44 K	45 J	46 T		
47 H	48 Y	49 V	50 O	51 M	52 D	53 N	54 E	55 U	56 R	57 O
58 N	59 P	60 F	61 C	62 J	63 B	64 O	65 A	66 R	67 B	
68 Q	69 Q	70 A	71 S	72 M	73 A	74 J	75 H	76 Q		
77 G	78 H	79 B	80 C	81 G	82 V	83 X	84 T	85 A	86 U	
87 Y	88 W	89 M	90 Y	91 H	92 S	93 O	94 L	95 M	96 N	
97 F	98 S	99 Q	100 B	101 J	102 O	103 I	104 T	105 G	106 T	
107 F	108 U	109 I	110 C	111 R	112 Q	113 L	114 N	115 D	116 S	
117 N	118 L	119 M	120 F	121 T	122 W	123 O	124 M	125 B	126 X	
127 Q	128 I	129 V	130 X	131 E	132 H	133 Y	134 S	135 B	136 Z	
137 W	138 N	139 B	140 M	141 S	142 P	143 R	144 X	145 V	146 F	
147 C	148 E	149 M	150 Z	151 B	152 H	153 T	154 N	155 D		
156 Q	157 M	158 Q	159 F	160 C	161 H	162 G	163 N	164 E	165 F	
166 W	167 N	168 A	169 E	170 Y	171 K	172 B	173 S	174 E		
175 P	176 V	177 B	178 S	179 X	180 J	181 E	182 V	183 R		
184 K	185 S	186 Q	187 L	188 X	189 T	190 G	191 I	192 F	193 N	
194 X	195 F	196 B	197 N	198 H	199 A	200 Q	201 D	202 Z	203 S	
204 T	205 S	206 B	207 A	208 D	209 E	210 S	211 E	212 H		
213 Y	214 J	215 C	216 G	217 R	218 H	219 X	220 F	221 W	222 V	
223 O	224 V	225 N	226 L	227 Z	228 G					

No. 42

CLUES

A. "I've a mouth like an old _____" (Kipling, "Cells") — 56 142 159 72 22 127

B. Most severe — 131 43 137 104 3 27 12

C. Vessel for Lipton, e.g. — 171 144 125 78 21

D. Game of chance — 150 64 90 68 94

E. "To the _____": Virginia Woolf novel — 10 141 93 20 52 123 46 173 156 55

F. Article of exercise equipment (2 wds.) — 5 138 118 75 9 61 82 195 106 29

G. Tough, hard — 129 89 45 14 35

H. "A fellow almost _____ in a fair wife" (contr., "Othello") — 99 178 190 108 146

I. Carefree — 163 110 101 23 18 32 185 67 8 122

J. State of being midway between two extremes — 194 98 166 112 120

K. Less — 71 168 192 115 181 95 184

L. Case, circumstance — 26 6 79 42 182

M. Suite — 177 136 130 60 76 39 198

N. Dandy, swell (chiefly Brit.) — 140 17 84 119

O. Refuge — 66 116 2 149 179

P. French bistro or small cafe — 7 183 148 102 160 187 143 54 24

Q. Jess Willard took the heavyweight championship away from him in 1915 (full name) — 38 147 86 53 30 11 25 51 128 13 103

R. Large ape of Borneo and Sumatra — 158 121 124 47 165 88 135 50 107

S. One of Joe DiMaggio's sobriquets (2 wds.) — 59 100 169 162 41 31 49 145 151 80 87 176 126

T. Toad-stabber — 70 16 85 186

U. Seaport, NW Belgium — 172 199 65 37 92 97

V. Stout fabric; inflated or turgid language — 57 28 197 155 48 81 157

W. Made slender or fine — 161 44 15 153 117 196 113 63 191 74

X. Yielding (2 wds.) — 175 109 40 154 152 4 1 188

Y. Caused by the treatment of a physician — 69 139 77 105 34 62 167 174 91 114

Z. Stingy — 134 83 111 189 193 36 58 180 96 170

Z₁. Plant with usu. blue, sometimes yellow, white, or red flowers — 19 132 73 33 133 96 164

No. 43

CLUES

WORDS

A Dance based on a promenade . . . 97 156 34 85 169 101 200 81

B Son of Laius and Jocasta 185 160 46 171 61 146 43

C Fr. department, cap. Lyons 124 195 205 8 187

D Judgment, opinion 193 131 194 215 89 163 207 28 99 10

E Commercial seaport, E co. Cork, Ireland 161 70 91 128 150 35 67

F Seeking victory by delay and harassment rather than decisive battle 206 213 48 158 130 127

G 1917 George M. Cohan song (2 wds.) 2 159 123 203 178 117 14 80 76

H 1959 Ionesco play 184 148 93 122 90 190 42 104 24 60

I Blast the ear 137 18 191 69 57 108

J "The worm / Mounts through all ___ of form" (2 wds.; Emerson, "May Day") 141 6 68 174 183 105 39 138 26

K Sound, fit 50 59 38 199 73 11

L Scarlet pimpernel 177 78 103 66 144 126 134 170 72

M "Youth on ___; and Pleasure at the helm" (2 wds.; Gray, "The Bard") 157 143 22 175 88 12 77

N Notorious 40 182 33 20 192 145 135 25

O The Chimera and the Minotaur, e.g. 94 153 63 186 5 189 71 19

P Discomposure; overabundance . . 31 102 188 198 58 154 211 165 17 113 167 98

Q Differently 176 132 27 217 3 54 65 92 82

R "He had ___ boxes, all carefully packed" (hyph.; Carroll, "Hunting of the Snark") . . . 152 87 56 142 180 129 49 79

S Deplored; wept 16 7 29 209 45 112 47 168

T Angel of death (Jewish and Islamic angelology) 9 214 120 202 53 109

U Sap 121 41 139 162 114 210 140 13 196

V Idols (2 wds.) 212 125 44 21 173 100 136 201 166 147 118 115

W Pagan 197 15 107 111 208 151 75

X Difficult, risky 172 51 106 204 32 119 84 37

Y Project 110 216 116 4 164 95 23 181 64 74

Z Argue, object 179 133 155 62 86 30 36 83 96 52 55

						1 P	2 G	3 Q	4 Y
		5 O	6 J	7 S	8 C				
9 T	10 D	11 K	12 M	13 U	14 G	15 W	16 S	17 P	18 I
19 O	20 N	21 N	22 M	23 Y	24 H	25 W	26 J	27 P	
28 D	29 S	30 Z	31 P	32 X	33 N	34 A	35 E	36 Z	37 X
39 J	40 N	41 U	42 H	43 B	44 V	45 S	46 B	47 S	38 K
48 F	49 R	50 K	51 X	52 X	53 T	54 Q	55 Z	56 R	
57 I	58 P	59 K	60 H	61 B	62 Z	63 O	64 Y	65 Y	66 L 67 E
68 J	69 I	70 E	71 O	72 L	73 K	74 Y	75 W	76 G	
77 M	78 L	79 R	80 G	81 A	82 Q	83 Z	84 X	85 A	86 Z
87 R	88 M	89 D	90 H	91 E	92 Q	93 H	94 O	95 Y	96 Z 97 A
98 P	99 D	100 V	101 A	102 P	103 L	104 H	105 J	106 X	107 W
108 I	109 Y	110 Y	111 W	112 S	113 P	114 U	115 V	116 Y	117 G
118 V	119 X	120 T	121 U	122 H	123 G	124 C	125 V	126 L	127 F 128 E
129 R	130 F	131 D	132 Q	133 Z	134 L	135 N	136 V	137 I	138 J
139 U	140 F	141 J	142 R	143 M	144 L	145 N	146 B	147 V	148 H
149 K	150 E	151 W	152 R	153 O	154 P	155 Z	156 A	157 M	158 F
159 G	160 B	161 E	162 U	163 D	164 Y	165 P	166 V	167 P	168 S
169 A	170 L	171 B	172 X	173 V	174 J	175 M	176 Q	177 L	178 G
179 Z	180 R	181 Y	182 N	183 J	184 H	185 B	186 O	187 C	188 P 189 O
190 H	191 H	192 N	193 D	194 D	195 C	196 U	197 W	198 P	199 K
200 A	201 V	202 T	203 G	204 X	205 C	206 F	207 D	208 W	209 S
210 U	211 P	212 V	213 F	214 T	215 D	216 Y	217 Q		

No. 44

CLUES

WORDS

A. Put out, doused . . . .
165 31 156 96 146 185 49 103 51 102 67 13

B. Eng. writer (1660?–1731;
"Robinson Crusoe") . . . .
94 173 91 38 84

C. Pademelon, e.g. . . . .
135 128 109 119 178 40 46

D. Wealthy . . . .
76 86 48 19 3 82 104 63

E. Whale shark . . . .
88 78 74 114 71 154 122 58 17

F. Series of events having vivid,
striking images; play . . . .
29 187 93 172 10

G. Has a certain value . . . .
199 170 155 57 65 75

H. Gangs . . . .
32 110 164 153 182

I. Checks, holds back . . . .
100 45 133 137 193 64 108 35

J. Expression of despair (2 wds.) . .
126 151 143 23 28

K. Japanese syllabic writing . . . . .
56 7 69 176

L. Act of choosing . . . .
197 54 149 92 81 14 107 121

M. Rigorously just and severe . . . .
80 99 22 112 12 89 72 117 198 61 5 163 166

N. Round painting or relief . . . . . .
147 79 111 95 192

O. Pulitzer Prize-winning musical
comedy, 1932 (4 wds.) . . . .
18 157 175 161 124 9 37 15 53 196 118

P. Leading characters at many a
reception . . . .
184 116 60 150 171 132 97 131 139

Q. 1922 Eliot work (2 wds. after
The) . . . .
59 136 70 127 186 169 62 27 115

R. Simple element of a compound
eye . . . .
26 66 123 130 144 183 41 43

S. Haphazard . . . .
159 113 174 190 2 179

T. Gangs of murderous robbers of
India and Burma . . . .
189 125 160 142 25 42 177

U. Bundle of rods borne before an
ancient Roman magistrate of
high grade . . . .
21 195 77 106 34 181

V. —— trouvés, in modern art . . .
145 141 191 180 138 50

W. Bay horses, flecked with gray,
e.g. . . . .
8 152 16 83 4

X. Hunter, trapper, camper, outdoor
type . . . .
98 47 90 20 105 194 44 39

Y. One who believes in mob rule . .
134 101 148 129 158 11 33 140 52

Z. Archangel who warns Adam of
Satan's presence in Paradise
("Paradise Lost") . . . .
6 162 168 24 68 30 55

Z₁. Last judgment . . . .
85 188 87 167 36 73 120 1

7	Z₁ 2	S 3	D	W 5	M 6	Z
K 8	W 9	O	10 F	1 Z₁	11 Y	12	S 3	D	W 5	M 6	Z

(Grid of numbered/lettered squares)

No. 45

CLUES

		WORDS
A	Moves at an easy gallop.	63 13 189 1 69 105 52
B	Best.	176 106 102 8 74 19 133
C	The real thing (after *The*)	47 101 197 194 145 192 178
D	Secured (2 wds.)	10 200 164 5 57
E	Uncertain, torn	15 25 65 84 151 50 92 127 113 71
F	Using high-flown, bombastic language	68 20 132 154 168 111 14 150 186 54 86 160 155
G	Handbook, manual	158 183 62 119 153 12 159 43 169 104 137
H	Make over	81 204 95 115 24 162
I	Cheap, sleazy	55 90 173 117 38 135
J	Shaft for Tashtego, Queequeg, or Daggoo, e.g.	78 37 97 80 182 11 131
K	Chosen.	188 134 67 44 33
L	Saddens	138 29 60 199 152 6 18 144 121
M	Project	100 123 110 96 147 126 143 46 161 3
N	Most frail or ineffectual	174 66 198 125 83 122 148 205 17
O	Undeveloped, rudimentary. . . .	82 59 56 45 35 23 116 202 103
P	Wait on.	64 195 7 40 70 30
Q	'Tho' marriage makes man and wife one flesh, it leaves 'em still ____" (2 wds.; Congreve, "The Double Dealer, Epistle Dedicatory")	28 118 107 89 79 193 51 129
R	N.Y. river formed by the Oneida and the Seneca	130 114 77 191 142 120
S	Attractive, charming	88 42 146 16 196 26 76 98
T	Fix	163 49 22 2 32 175
U	Not plain-spoken; insincere (hyph).	9 75 139 171 93 4 112 187 27 179 165 85
V	One who tries to influence a jury illegally.	73 177 34 201 109 190 94 99
W	Strolls about idly	128 141 157 53 72 61 184
X	Principally (3 wds.)	58 167 140 36 185 203 172 48 170
Y	Short-barreled rifle	181 166 108 91 124 31 21
Z	Forcefully, vigorously	87 149 136 156 41

No. 46

CLUES

A Dilapidated as Heep was to a small degree in town . . . . .
    208 148 132 24 185 113 50 181 104 93

B Fans badgers? . . . . .
    167 122 211 144 175 118

C . . . and German tower broken flow. . . . .
    174 206 42 74 123 160 58 51

D Red yeoman going to get year's first available wealth (2 wds.). . . . .
    130 85 197 26 147 200 103 82 61 170

E Fool party returning second shocker (2 wds.). . . . .
    157 98 124 171 23 65 48 94 140 151

F Inciting a Conservative after Elizabeth I cracked thorax . . . . .
    21 107 165 39 117 57 83 194 128 18

G Musician's Chinaman breaking in or returning very loudly to musicians. . . . .
    60 10 88 52 91 159 192 205 101 32 129 182

H Politeness truly begins and ends after 101, 6, and 51. . . . . .
    198 141 20 193 120 195 180 109

I One with skill in part is thoughtful . . . . .
    116 9 204 134 196 164

J A girl gets mixed up with more involved procedure . . . . .
    38 55 36 99 143 133 81 49 68

K They get plucked by intricate hip-fastener . . . . .
    59 34 137 110 92 37 12 5 166 203 56

L Gamine solved riddle . . . . .
    45 35 13 163 76 89

M Anais pines badly for game . . . . .
    64 136 90 127 8 150 162 29

N Shelley Duvall played the film role of "Io, Lovely Screwball" (2 wds.) . . . . .
    210 17 31 187 73 2 27 169

O Antagonist, losing little worker, goes wild after cat starts taking it easy . . . . .
    11 191 176 135 66 80 95 145

P Macho wit, so deft in a way (hyph.) . . . . .
    108 97 178 71 77 7 115 156

Q Name the ingredient; it leavens . . . . .
    186 153 4 70 43 125 172

R Birds on Homer's new version. . . . . .
    84 202 119 30 67 184 149 105

S Considering moving lift on height (4 wds.). . . . .
    161 41 183 213 100 16 28 138 44 33 199 69

T Blooming finger broken about base. . . . .
    201 79 168 46 158 146 190 75 212

U Irish port for Falstaff's young friend Henry, having lost his center. . . . .
    114 25 139 207 209 15 78

V Exaggerate undercover dossier's features. . . . .
    152 112 63 22 126 131

W Divine nut, cracked, wasn't asked. . . . .
    179 155 106 142 62 87 72 19 121

X Southern character from Ponca Junction . . . . .
    14 154 173 40 1

Y Draws a tumbler of Grant's . . . . .
    6 3 53 86 96 189

Z Flitting from East to West with an Italian economist . . . . .
    102 188 214 54 111

WORDS

No. 47

CLUES | WORDS

Clue		WORDS
A	Mimicked (2 wds.)	138 77 103 25 108 83 178
B	Extended.	88 169 73 80 147 182 52 142 32 172 157 44
C	Off-color.	127 28 47 20 95 123
D	Noisy commotion	114 91 18 58 31 133
E	Titular hero of an unfinished Dickensian work (2 wds.)	33 171 99 72 105 8 121 2 56 41
F	"Here's a ___ devil here, / That commonly rebels" (3 wds., "Othello").	13 94 46 170 181 63 4 30 162 71 132 43 155 36 40 102
G	Scorching.	112 164 140 146 98 15
H	Balderdash, piffle.	76 60 151 119 129 87 74
I	Symbolic devices.	153 90 22 48 166 70 189
J	Say in reply; retort.	152 141 81 23 104 66
K	Son of Agamemnon and Clytemnestra.	168 86 176 137 185 144 148
L	Lies heavy upon.	125 167 1 135 38 159 175 118 188
M	Locks.	75 10 136 93 111 161 134
N	In such a manner that (2 wds.)	17 113 100 50
O	Establishing; appointing.	120 19 53 79 65 97 69 186 126
P	Great fastball pitcher for Cleveland, 1936–56.	37 14 177 29 115 165
Q	Type of restaurant (hyph.).	130 54 64 26 180 78
R	Wandered over, ranged	160 57 184 61 110 5
S	Repetition of the same word or phrases in several successive clauses.	85 45 9 131 39 62 42 139 109 16
T	Distill, esp. in an old-fashioned way.	12 35 82 174 55 96 59 7 179 128
U	Simple, hardy, laconic, frugal, brave.	101 21 154 11 107 145 89
V	"Let us not always say / 'Spite ___ today'" (3 wds.; Browning, "Rabbi ben Ezra")	150 84 124 51 173 92 27 122 183 158 117
W	"___ on Life, Death, and Immortality" (2 wds.): poem by Edward Young.	156 49 67 6 163 116 68 24 3 106 143 149 34

Grid

1 L	2 E	3 W	4 F	5 R	■	6 W	7 T	8 E	9 S	
10 M	11 U	12 T	13 F	14 F	15 G	16 S	17 N	18 D	19 O	
20 C	21 U	22 I	23 J	24 W	25 A	26 Q	27 V	28 C	29 P	
30 F	31 D	32 B	33 E	34 W	■	35 T	36 F	37 P	38 L	
39 S	40 F	41 E	42 S	43 F	44 B	45 S	46 F	47 C	48 C	
49 W	50 N	51 V	52 B	53 O	54 Q	55 T	56 E	57 R	58 D	
59 T	60 H	61 R	62 S	63 F	64 Q	65 O	66 J	67 W	68 W	
69 O	70 I	71 F	72 E	73 B	74 H	75 M	76 H	77 A	78 Q	
79 O	80 B	81 J	82 T	83 A	84 V	85 S	86 K	87 K	88 B	89 U
90 I	91 D	92 V	93 M	94 F	95 C	96 T	97 O	98 G	99 E	
100 N	101 U	102 F	103 A	104 J	105 E	106 W	107 U	108 A		
109 S	110 R	111 M	112 G	113 N	114 D	115 P	116 W	117 V	118 L	
119 H	120 O	121 E	122 V	123 C	124 V	125 L	126 O	127 C	128 T	
129 H	130 Q	131 S	132 F	133 D	134 M	135 L	136 M	137 K	138 A	139 S
140 G	141 J	142 B	143 W	144 K	145 U	146 G	147 B	148 K		
149 W	150 V	151 H	152 J	153 I	154 U	155 F	156 W	157 B	158 V	159 L
160 R	161 M	162 F	163 W	164 G	165 P	166 I	167 L	168 K	169 B	
170 F	171 E	172 B	173 V	174 T	175 L	176 K	177 P	178 A	179 T	
180 Q	181 F	182 B	183 V	184 R	185 K	186 O	187 Q	188 L	189 I	

No. 48

CLUES

A Trinket — 32 142 17 105 125 139

B Out for a good time (3 wds.) — 114 70 168 33 135 150 128 11 156

C Sudden increase of depth in a large body of water — 146 97 116 123 16 10 65 161

D Regular; lawful — 144 31 88

E Contrary; refractory — 102 28 147 111 1 67 120 53

F Sway — 119 26 86 25 46

G Form into an arch — 61 51 3 155 56

H Inherent ability — 4 39 24 163 153 113 64 104 95

I In some countries, a legislative assembly — 110 94 42 145

J Unspoken — 92 169 76 124 60

K Yearn — 138 55 118 38 63 84

L "An ___ may be cross'd in love" (Sheridan, "The Critic") — 159 2 83 41 14 154

M Worker who has learned a handicraft or trade — 47 23 108 136 101 127 73 37 12 68

N Not voguish (3 wds.) — 36 45 141 107 162 82 165 66 72 98

O But seriously—(2 wds.) — 91 30 171 19 35 49 131 89 157

P Legendary king of Sweden, who could direct the wind by turning his cap — 140 13 103 80

Q Fastest — 170 106 90 59 74 81 148 34

R Song of praise or devotion — 69 6 126 166 52 22

S Evil; depraved — 130 5 20 75 79 8 99

T Rave; rhapsodize (colloq.) — 100 62 54 151 93 85 112

U O.K. — 164 121 50 57 129

V Invention; creation; composition — 117 48 158 29 15 115 43 21 96 77

W Furrow, channel — 7 78 160 44 134 167

X Brain — 149 9 132 152 122 87 71 109 58 143

Y Bundle — 137 18 133 40 27

Diagram

1 E	2 L	3 G	4 H	5 S	6 R	7 W	8 S	9 X	10 C	11 B	12 M	13 P	14 L	15 V	16 C
17 A	18 Y	19 O	20 S	21 V	22 R	23 M	24 H	25 F	26 F						
27 Y	28 E	29 V	30 O	31 D	32 A	33 B	34 Q	35 O	36 N						
37 M	38 K	39 H	40 Y	41 L	42 I	43 V	44 W	45 N	46 F						
47 M	48 V	49 O	50 U	51 G	52 R	53 E	54 T	55 K	56 G	57 U					
58 X	59 Q	60 J	61 G	62 T	63 K	64 H	65 C	66 N							
67 E	68 M	69 R	70 B	71 X	72 N	73 M	74 Q	75 S	76 J						
77 V	78 W	79 S	80 P	81 Q	82 N	83 L	84 K	85 T	86 F	87 X					
88 D	89 O	90 Q	91 O	92 J	93 T	94 I	95 H	96 V	97 C	98 N					
99 S	100 T	101 M	102 E	103 P	104 H	105 A	106 Q	107 N	108 M						
109 X	110 I	111 E	112 T	113 H	114 B	115 V	116 C	117 V							
118 K	119 F	120 E	121 U	122 X	123 C	124 J	125 A	126 R	127 M	128 B					
129 U	130 S	131 O	132 X	133 Y	134 W	135 B	136 M	137 Y	138 K						
139 A	140 P	141 N	142 A	143 X	144 D	145 I	146 C								
147 E	148 Q	149 X	150 B	151 T	152 X	153 H	154 L	155 G	156 B						
157 O	158 V	159 L	160 W	161 C	162 N	163 H	164 U	165 N							
166 R	167 W	168 B	169 J	170 Q	171 O										

No. 49

CLUES

WORDS

A Inadequate. 169 92 78 146

B Cortisone and epinephrine, e.g. . 72 94 172 83 110 135 128 68

C Sturdy fabric used in men's
clothing (2 wds.) 67 103 25 126 164 147 1 108 81 40

D Pleasing, genial 119 20 26 64 161 123 50 132

E Reciprocal effect 87 157 30 57 74 61 93 59 125 36 39

F "To wring / From the hard hands
of ___ their vile trash" ("Julius
Caesar") 121 167 11 100 16 138 118 52

G Hacks; conforms, adheres 131 48 159 163

H Type of network deployed by
most feminists (2 wds.). 158 124 58 109 45 35

I To the full amount or extent . . 80 149 42 13 89 76

J Recluse, hermit 82 117 5 19 106 142 98 130 33

K Dining hall in a monastery,
convent, college, etc. 43 150 144 2 139 66 3 79 17

L Challenge. 129 145 77 120

M Lacking courage or determination
(hyph.). 151 134 38 166 156 21 73 143 62

N Charms. 137 10 86 75 171 96 115 32 56

O With constant and careful
attention 165 23 155 141 91 55 97 37 162 12 112

P Catch in a gunlock that holds
the hammer cocked. 71 29 90 113

Q Pre-revolutionary name of
Montmorency, France 69 34 22 127 8 116 160

R Unrestraint. 24 9 148 105 101 85 173 133 15

S Furcula. 47 154 7 152 28 60 95 170

T Bars, bans 84 122 18 49 6 31 99

U Trust, confidence 65 140 88 41 70 46 4 27

V Roundabout; not straightforward. 111 114 63 53 102 168

W Methods, procedures 104 14 44 136 51 107 54

Grid

1 C	2 K	3 K	4 U	5 J	6 T	7 S			
8 Q	9 R	10 N	11 F	12 O	13 I	14 W	15 R	16 F	17 K
18 T	19 J	20 D	21 M	22 Q	23 O	■	24 R	25 C	26 D	27 U
28 S	29 P	30 E	31 T	32 N	33 J	34 Q	35 H	36 E	37 O
38 M	39 E	40 C	41 U	42 I	43 K	44 W	45 H	46 U	
47 S	48 G	49 T	50 D	51 W	52 F	53 V	54 W	55 O	56 N
57 E	58 H	59 E	60 S	61 E	62 M	63 V	64 D	65 U	66 K
67 C	68 B	69 Q	70 U	71 P	72 B	73 M	74 E	75 N	76 I
77 L	78 A	79 K	80 I	81 C	82 J	83 B	84 T	85 R	
86 N	87 N	88 U	89 I	90 P	91 O	92 A	93 E	94 B	95 S	96 N
97 O	98 J	99 T	100 F	101 R	102 V	103 C	104 W	105 R	106 J	107 W
108 C	109 H	110 B	111 V	112 O	113 P	114 V	115 N	116 Q	117 J	118 F
119 D	120 L	121 F	122 T	123 D	124 H	125 E	126 C	127 Q	128 B	129 L
130 J	131 G	132 D	133 R	134 M	135 B	136 W	137 N	138 F	139 K
140 U	141 O	142 J	143 M	144 K	145 L	146 A	147 C	148 R	
149 I	150 K	151 M	152 S	153 V	154 S	155 O	156 M		
157 E	158 H	159 G	160 Q	161 D	162 O	163 G	164 C	165 O	166 M
167 F	168 V	169 A	170 S	171 N	172 B	173 R			

No. 50

Acrostic puzzle grid (numbered cells 1–183 with clue-letter designations; black squares separate words).

CLUES — WORDS

A Defeating utterly . . . .
131 173 156 163 135 83 34

B Not prudent or discreet . . . .
69 20 126 75 165 149 146 139 101

C Beats, as a heart or pulse . . . . . .
30 180 16 8 37 51

D Unsound; fleeting; deceptive; empty . . . .
104 130 88 53 28 43

E Grasp . . . .
133 47 29 31 111 72

F Seaport, NW Belgium . . . .
42 128 147 19 98 7

G Lacking; type of poster, esp. in post offices . . . . .
4 25 91 103 73 110

H Join; add . . . . . .
81 58 71 48 94 120

I "A votary of the desk — a ____ and cropt scrivener" (Lamb, "Oxford in the Vacation") . . .
50 10 119 87 115 179 176

J Intended . . . .
41 85 35 175 24

K Threatening . . . .
113 182 62 140 96 174 170

L Corrected . . . .
172 168 39 142 148 46 137

M Genus of S American plants with fragrant white flowers . . . .
143 82 60 45 161 36 57 155

N Stiff, lifeless; insensitive . . . . .
56 95 122 21 109 159

O Mean; snivy; feisty . . . . . .
15 65 154 108 123 55

P The painting of unworthy or sordid subjects . . . . . .
86 61 74 129 171 100 102 160 93 118 52 134 106

Q Have understanding of . . . . . .
97 67 153 14

R Without force . . . .
107 151 13 68 112 27

S Indolent; futile . . . .
99 18 164 92 12 66

T Oblique angled parallelogram with only the opposite sides equal . .
125 178 23 1 117 76 166 84

U Expression of guiding principle . .
157 6 132 22 78

V Surpassed in cunning . . . .
145 11 167 49 158 141 177 121 64

W "The women are foolish: God Almighty made 'em ____" (4 wds.; Eliot, "Adam Bede") . . . . .
44 181 150 54 70 162 59 79 5 2 144 33 127

X Comblike instrument for separating the fibers of flax, hemp, etc. . .
9 90 152 26 136 183

Y Understanding or agreement, as between nations . . . .
40 77 124 89 3 114 105

Z Dissolute, debauched man . . . . .
138 38 17 169 32 116 63 80

No. 51

CLUES / WORDS

A. Of or like a tail 69 2 102 12 75 154

B. Custom; disposition. 114 84 166 1 176 79 120

C. Order of lizards of which the tuatara is the only survivor.   19 77 151 76 66 193 117 129 33

D. "Go out ___ and hedges, and compel them to come in" (3 wds., Luke 14:23). .   61 93 40 81 55 175 24 124 160 149 157 4 106 82 183 185 192

E. Bask.   131 42 107

F. City in the Snake River valley, S Idaho (2 wds.)   7 184 147 103 20 162 182 196 91

G. Declining, decreasing (3 wds.)   171 60 22 8 14 156 72 190 153

H. Central point   105 96 88 27 16

I. Laugh in scorn, mirth, etc.   180 78 111 195

J. River, NW Germany, flowing into the North Sea   139 3 51

K. Former great player for the Montréal Canadiens, nick-named "the Rocket".   189 35 94 32 11 101 146

L. Heath.   52 165 49 90

M. Social function; matter.   130 74 45 38 9 80

N. Play adaptation by Colton and Randolph from Maugham's "Miss Thompson"   34 136 127 85

O. Describe   73 92 150 164

P. 1947 Carol Reed film starring James Mason (3 wds.)   44 108 163 29 98 13 133 54 179

Q. Hearty, sincere, earnest.   62 97 41 119 18 126 87 6 28 31 194 86

R. Gr. version of Aurora.   37 30 152

S. "The deep ___ of prodigious breasts" (Swinburne, "Ave atque Vale")   168 15 99 173 65 191 53 148

T. Raging; fanatical or unreasonably zealous.   68 21 187 48 83

U. Great Scottish estuary, anc. Bodotria (3 wds.)   155 178 25 123 58 110 172 134 188 5 125 71

V. Flooded with water.   67 121 181 141 23

W. Ailing.   144 159 57 115 36 47

X. Show derision or scorn, esp. by facial expression.   186 145 132 158 140

Y. Convolute; interlace.   170 177 122 112 70

Z. King Arthur was his illegitimate son (full name)   104 113 56 89 135 39 100 50 109 118 46 174 143 26

Z₁. "But seas do laugh, when rocks are near" (2 wds.; Webster, "The White Devil")   64 17 167 142 116 161 138 43 59

Diagram (cell number · clue-letter)

9 M		1 B	2 A	3 J		4 D	5 U	6 Q	7 F	8 G
19 C		10 C	11 K	12 A	13 P		14 G	15 S	16 H	17 Z₁ 18 Q
29 P	20 F	21 T	22 G	23 V	24 D	25 U	26 Z	27 H	28 Q	
38 M	30 R	31 Q	32 K	33 C	34 N	35 K		36 W	37 R	
47 W	39 Z	40 D	41 Q	42 E	43 Z₁	44 P	45 M	46 Z		
57 W	48 T	49 L	50 Z	51 J	52 L	53 S	54 P	55 D	56 Z	
65 S	58 U	59 Z₁	60 G	61 D	62 Q	63 D	64 Z₁			
75 A	66 C	67 V	68 T	69 A	70 Y	71 U	72 G	73 O	74 M	
84 B	76 C	77 C	78 I	79 B	80 M	81 D	82 D	83 T		
94 K	85 N	86 Q	87 Q	88 H	89 Z	90 L	91 F	92 O	93 D	
103 F	95 C	96 H	97 Q	98 P	99 S	100 Z	101 K	102 A		
112 Y	104 Z	105 H	106 D	107 E	108 P	109 Z	110 U	111 I		
121 V	113 Z	114 B	115 W	116 Z₁	117 C	118 Z	119 Q	120 B		
131 E	122 Y	123 U	124 D	125 U	126 Q	127 N	128 D	129 C	130 M	
141 V	132 X	133 P	134 U	135 Z	136 N	137 C	138 Z₁	139 J	140 X	
151 C	142 Z₁	143 Z	144 W	145 X	146 K	147 F	148 S	149 D	150 O	
161 Z₁	152 R	153 G	154 A	155 U	156 G	157 D	158 X	159 W	160 D	
170 Y	162 F	163 P	164 O	165 L	166 B	167 Z₁	168 S	169 S		
180 I	171 G	172 U	173 S	174 Z	175 D	176 B	177 Y	178 U	179 P	
189 K	181 V	182 F	183 C	184 F	185 C	186 X	187 T	188 U		
190 G	191 S	192 C	193 C	194 Q	195 I	196 F				

No. 52

CLUES

WORDS

A City in central Yorkshire, England . . . . — 14 79 9 42 118

B Considering (3 wds.) . . . . . — 102 34 121 89 191 44 175 143

C Surfeits. . . . . — 183 200 31 25 100

D Singer Billie, born Eleanora Fagan (1915–59) . . . . . . — 133 17 111 60 126 86

E Drifts, bents . . . . . . — 83 23 174 113 189 62 156 136 99 29

F "Then the lover, / Sighing like ____, with a woeful ballad" ("As You Like It") — 196 2 199 40 85 63 171

G Access; unrestricted opportunity (2 wds.) . . — 168 187 61 91 73 181 195 39

H "____ forget: yet all shall be forgot, / But he'll remember with advantages" (2 wds, "Henry V") — 153 120 75 76 33 80

I Something spectacular, entertaining, full of confused action (hyph. and wd.) . . . . — 184 8 103 27 166 48 149 56 197 59 4 78 94 16 159

J Berets' relatives . . . . — 88 164 70 105

K Final stages of an undertaking. . . . . — 157 49 51 170 98 7 3 144 161 132 185

L Amuses; harbors, considers . — 64 82 128 41 97 163 142 177 135 190

M Name of six kings of Sweden — 101 13 123 35 45 193 96 179

N Inappropriate, unsuitable (3 wds.) . . . . . . — 95 38 15 77 47 129 192 141 112 148

O Glance or wink; ogle . . . . . — 90 69 26 110 180 52 67 194

P Judges, thinks, believes. . . . — 32 116 74 12 138

Q Places of retreat or asylum. . — 115 65 22 131 107 19

R Uninformed . . . . — 87 6 24 173 188 139 72 53

S The full extent of anything . — 151 55 50 18 37

T Am. writer (1894–1961), creator of Nick Charles and Sam Spade . . . . . . — 167 71 130 176 106 10 114

U Precipitation; haste . . . . . . — 58 11 68 57 122 140 125 21 201 155

V Large flightless ratite bird of Australia, New Guinea, etc. . — 137 92 28 36 162 145 43 108 154

W Roman poet and satirist (65–8 B.C.) . . . . — 54 158 84 147 178 119

X The devil (2 wds.) . . . . . . — 109 93 1 150 124 172 165

Y Government official who investigates citizens' complaints against the government . . . . — 81 117 152 127 146 20 169 134 66

Z Merciful, indulgent . . . . . . — 104 160 5 198 186 182 30

No. 53

CLUES / WORDS

A. Shelves 138 199 146 18 188 145

B. Inefficient; lazy 41 201 191 161 133 73 21 177 107

C. Linguistic form from which another form is historically derived 8 168 197 119 186 14

D. Chemical-warfare agent, characterized by its vesicant action 37 64 49 130 190 95 71 24

E. Dress worn by Muslim pilgrims to Mecca 60 151 129 123 198

F. Wide of the mark; all wet (2 wds.) 182 84 110 22 118 45 79

G. Deal with; discuss 48 128 13 65 63

H. Governing bodies 155 97 66 62 75 139 44

I. Bosses who underpay and overwork their employees 159 136 105 147 57 170 11 25

J. Atoll comprising forty islets in the W Carolines 166 17 127 184 134 39

K. Teases, heckles 142 51 103 12 78 87 70

L. Small, pointed implements for making holes in the ground for planting seeds, etc. 67 69 167 77 2 40 112

M. 22nd state of the U.S. 31 193 137 46 1 59 43

N. Falstaff calls Dombledon, "a rascally knave" (hyph.; "Henry IV, Part 2") 106 47 154 89 195 189 56 121 160 81 173

O. Island whose cap. is Valletta 124 192 38 120 58

P. In general (3 wds.) 3 131 28 149 36 101 117 88 169 157

Q. Seamlike union between two parts of an organ or the like 114 16 42 29 99

R. Something that induces a pleasurable forgetfulness 104 50 94 23 4 126 7 92

S. Perception, grasp 85 98 171 27 5 54 19

T. Spiritual renascence (2 wds.) 183 55 15 35 72 33 111 20

U. Go free; begin; publish (2 wds.) 9 102 200 175 83 113

V. Overly facile 165 109 116 194 176 144 80 148 141 86

W. Moral significance 135 162 122 115 125

X. Tramp slang for r.r. train 179 10 90 150 196 164 185

Y. Leguminous herbs cultivated for forage and soil improvement 187 76 53 96 163 180 100

Z. Looper 32 52 181 108 26 82 140 153

Z_1. Fraud, deception 172 30 152 74 156

Z_2. Scientific description of the races of the earth 93 6 91 61 174 132 158 178 68 143 34

Grid (cell number + clue letter, in reading order)

Row	Cells
1	1 M · 2 L · 3 P · 4 R · 5 S · 6 Z_2 · 7 R · 8 C · 9 U · 10 X
2	11 I · 12 K · 13 G · 14 C · 15 T · 16 Q · 17 J · 18 A · 19 S · 20 T · 21 B
3	22 F · 23 R · 24 D · 25 I · 26 Z · 27 S · 28 P · 29 Q · 30 Z_1
4	31 M · 32 Z · 33 T · 34 Z_2 · 35 T · 36 P · 37 D · 38 O · 39 J · 40 L · 41 B
5	42 Q · 43 M · 44 H · 45 F · 46 M · 47 N · 48 G · 49 D · 50 R · 51 K
6	52 Z · 53 Y · 54 S · 55 T · 56 N · 57 I · 58 O · 59 M · 60 E · 61 Z_2
7	62 H · 63 G · 64 D · 65 G · 66 H · 67 L · 68 Z_2 · 69 L · 70 K · 71 D
8	72 T · 73 H · 74 Z_1 · 75 H · 76 Y · 77 L · 78 K · 79 F · 80 V · 81 N
9	82 Z · 83 U · 84 F · 85 S · 86 V · 87 K · 88 P · 89 N · 90 X · 91 Z_2
10	92 R · 93 Z_2 · 94 R · 95 D · 96 Y · 97 H · 98 S · 99 Q · 100 Y · 101 P
11	102 U · 103 K · 104 R · 105 I · 106 N · 107 B · 108 Z · 109 V · 110 F · 111 T · 112 L
12	113 U · 114 Q · 115 W · 116 V · 117 P · 118 F · 119 C · 120 O · 121 N
13	122 W · 123 E · 124 O · 125 W · 126 R · 127 J · 128 G · 129 E · 130 D · 131 P
14	132 Z_2 · 133 B · 134 J · 135 W · 136 I · 137 M · 138 A · 139 H · 140 Z
15	141 V · 142 K · 143 Z_2 · 144 V · 145 A · 146 A · 147 A · 148 V · 149 P
16	150 X · 151 E · 152 Z_1 · 153 Z · 154 N · 155 H · 156 Z_1 · 157 P · 158 Z_2 · 159 I
17	160 N · 161 B · 162 W · 163 Y · 164 X · 165 V · 166 J · 167 L · 168 C · 169 P
18	170 I · 171 S · 172 Z_1 · 173 N · 174 Z_2 · 175 U · 176 V · 177 B · 178 Z_2 · 179 X
19	180 Y · 181 Z · 182 F · 183 T · 184 J · 185 X · 186 C · 187 Y · 188 A · 189 N · 190 D
20	191 B · 192 O · 193 M · 194 V · 195 N · 196 X · 197 C · 198 E · 199 A · 200 U · 201 B

No. 54

Grid

1 L	2 V	3 T	4 E	5 M	6 J	7 I

8 ■	9 D	10 A	11 R	12 F	13 Y	14 O	15 F	16 E	17 A
18 O	19 J	20 N	21 B	22 U	23 G	24 Q	25 P	26 N	27 G	28 F
29 K	30 N	31 X	32 T	33 H	34 Y	35 O	36 R	37 E	
38 R	39 H	40 F	41 N	42 U	43 Q	44 E	45 F	46 S	
47 H	48 D	49 C	50 V	51 L	52 F	53 C	54 N	55 K	56 G
57 J	58 A	59 R	60 S	61 P	62 W	63 K	64 J	65 Y	66 L
67 S	68 F	69 X	70 B	71 N	72 J	73 W	74 M	75 R	76 E
77 J	78 T	79 O	80 P	81 T	82 U	83 X	84 S	85 E	
86 J	87 H	88 U	89 E	90 Y	91 D	92 F	93 U	94 P	
95 V	96 B	97 O	98 R	99 K	100 Y	101 C	102 M	103 H	104 T
105 I	106 O	107 M	108 W	109 K	110 G	111 L	112 E	113 G	
114 V	115 P	116 B	117 V	118 J	119 X	120 B	121 L	122 V	
123 B	124 S	125 I	126 C	127 X	128 A	129 N	130 L	131 N	132 W	133 A
134 L	135 V	136 Q	137 Y	138 G	139 X	140 H	141 L	142 Y	
143 J	144 J	145 B	146 I	147 B	148 T	149 U	150 S	151 Q	
152 H	153 J	154 X	155 U	156 L	157 K	158 J	159 T	160 D	161 B
162 P	163 K	164 E	165 N	166 K	167 O	168 U	169 K	170 M	171 W
172 B	173 N	174 M	175 F	176 E	177 Q	178 W	179 O	180 P	181 M
182 C	183 X	184 V	185 T	186 F	187 R	188 U	

CLUES

A. V.P. of the U.S., 1925–29; winner 1925 Nobel peace prize . . . .
B. Weave . . . .
C. Treasury . . . .
D. Dog-salmon . . . .
E. Great, broad expanses . . . . . .
F. Crustacea, arachnids, millipedes, insects, etc. . . . .
G. Cipher . . . .
H. Notched; set as with teeth . . . . .
I. Small boat . . . .
J. Ignoramus; member of an Am. political party, 1853–56 (hyph.) . . . .
K. Embankment . . . .
L. "Man for the field and woman for ——," (2 wds.; Tennyson, "The Princess") . . . .
M. Goodness! Gracious! Upper regions . . . .
N. Right-angled . . . .
O. Carpenter's trestle for supporting wood . . . .
P. "The poor man had nothing, save one little ——" (2 wds., II Sam.: 1) . . . .
Q. Wild, untamed . . . .
R. Honest, just . . . .
S. Settle comfortably . . . .
T. Talking much about little . . . . .
U. Crystalline alkaloid also called corynine . . . .
V. Memento . . . .
W. Enmity (hyph.) . . . .
X. Topple . . . .
Y. Wrack, e.g. . . . .

WORDS

A. 133 9 17 128 58
B. 70 172 123 116 145 120 147 21 161 96
C. 126 53 182 49 101
D. 160 8 91 48
E. 4 176 85 76 37 89 164 16 44 112
F. 15 186 28 175 40 11 68 92 52 45
G. 138 110 27 23 113 56
H. 47 33 87 140 103 152 39
I. 7 125 105 146
J. 86 6 57 158 64 77 72 153 19 118 143
K. 163 169 99 29 109 55 157 166 63
L. 111 134 51 121 66 1 156 130 141
M. 102 5 174 170 181 74 107
N. 26 129 20 30 131 173 54 71 165 41
O. 35 106 14 79 179 18 97 167
P. 162 180 80 61 94 115 25
Q. 43 151 136 24 177
R. 98 59 10 36 75 38 187
S. 46 124 67 150 84 60
T. 159 185 104 78 3 148 144 32 81
U. 188 149 168 82 93 155 42 22 88
V. 50 114 122 184 2 117 95 135
W. 73 12 178 108 171 62 132
X. 139 31 119 127 83 69 183 154
Y. 90 65 137 34 100 142 13

No. 55

CLUES / WORDS

Clue		Words
A	Accent	57 4 157 40 22 114 66 54
B	Associates, partners; spouses	23 29 130 88 25 33 49 58 55 141 195
C	Handles	122 107 145 77 34
D	Properly, correctly	112 74 16 85 172 71
E	Most corrupt or unsound	144 190 127 8 7 81 63 100 138
F	Criticized or rebuked severely	119 48 143 189 61 182 13 140 6
G	Out of the question	174 147 39 180 19 70 135 199 75 184 116
H	Spur parts	95 151 181 10 14 155
I	Emits steady light	68 106 134 79 171
J	Area between head and abdomen	137 56 128 93 27 197
K	S American revolutionary and ruler of Chile (1778-1842)	133 153 80 175 1 185 97 52
L	Symbol of Scotland	28 65 89 168 60 105 111
M	Fiends, holy terrors	142 59 183 192 158 72 67 18
N	Jostles	99 150 203 12 115 24
O	Barrelhouse, gutbucket, e.g.	46 47 20 154 177 166 194 109 3
P	Loose, off-color	50 86 149 131 165 21
Q	Horrified	91 82 32 102 43 121
R	Old World warbler, *Sylvia communis*, e.g.	11 62 146 98 42 31 139 113 108 167 83
S	At once	104 17 162 64 136 30 118 132 193
T	Indomitable (hyph.)	191 51 36 164 159 78 5 120 198 69 170
U	Sparkled	176 26 45 38 161 123 92
V	Incidentally (3 wds.)	103 200 186 169 126 152 110
W	How herds of livestock are numbered (3 wds.)	73 124 90 125 37 9 202 84 163
X	Assistant professor in a French college	188 178 201 2 160 117 101
Y	At once (2 wds.)	173 76 148 41 53 44 187 179 94
Z	Roundabout	15 35 87 196 129 96 156

GRID

1 K	2 X	3 O	4 A	5 T	6 F	7 E	8 E		
9 W	10 H	11 R	12 N	13 F	14 H	15 Z	16 D	17 S	
18 M	19 G	20 O	21 P	22 A	23 B	24 N	25 B	26 U	27 J
28 L	29 B	30 S	31 R	32 Q	33 B	34 C	35 Z	36 T	
37 W	38 U	39 G	40 A	41 Y	42 R	43 Q	44 Y	45 U	46 O
47 O	48 F	49 B	50 P	51 T	52 K	53 Y	54 A	55 B	
56 J	57 A	58 B	59 M	60 L	61 F	62 R	63 E		
64 S	65 L	66 A	67 M	68 I	69 T	70 G	71 D	72 M	73 W
74 D	75 G	76 Y	77 C	78 T	79 I	80 K	81 E	82 Q	83 R
84 W	85 D	86 P	87 P	88 B	89 L	90 W	91 Q		
92 U	93 J	94 Y	95 H	96 Z	97 K	98 R	99 N	100 E	101 X
102 Q	103 V	104 S	105 L	106 I	107 C	108 R	109 O	110 V	111 L
112 D	113 R	114 A	115 N	116 G	117 X	118 S	119 F	120 T	
121 Q	122 C	123 U	124 W	125 W	126 V	127 E	128 J	129 Z	130 B
131 P	132 S	133 K	134 I	135 G	136 S	137 J	138 E		
139 R	140 F	141 B	142 M	143 M	144 E	145 C	146 R	147 G	148 Y
149 P	150 N	151 H	152 V	153 K	154 O	155 H	156 Z	157 A	158 M
159 T	160 X	161 U	162 S	163 W	164 T	165 P	166 O	167 R	168 L
169 V	170 T	171 I	172 D	173 Y	174 G	175 K	176 U	177 O	178 X
179 Y	180 G	181 H	182 F	183 S	184 H	185 K	186 V		
187 Y	188 X	189 F	190 E	191 T	192 M	193 S			
194 O	195 B	196 Z	197 J	198 T	199 G	200 V	201 X	202 W	203 N

No. 56

CLUES

WORDS

A Caned 99 149 35 185 175 125 39 97

B Frequent; place much frequented 104 155 79 4 53

C Choosing the best out of everything 147 159 131 105 81 32 166 11

D Acceptable to mind or feelings; pleasant to taste 153 84 182 75 90 72 212 14 5

E Am. playwright (1891–1939; "They Knew What They Wanted") 71 102 117 184 141 122

F The Brewster ladies' medium for arsenic in "Arsenic and Old Lace" (2 wds.) 60 146 10 126 206 24 136 210 119 45 103 138 178 116

G Works up (old material) in a new form 216 107 59 8 189 63 86 110

H Strip; take to bits; pull down 172 112 169 44 88 49 151 145 174

I Doubtful; shady 57 130 3 217 201

J Matchlessly 68 96 160 123 200 203 177 215 31 128 193 19

K Something a guitarist might do 55 124 192 98 38

L Wearisome 73 168 121 218 56 48 78

M Time to come 87 13 58 198 137 2 70 52

N Inadequately fed 191 36 34 188 106 113 118 211 82 41 202 176 140 197

O Ranunculaceous plant also called "devil-in-the-bush" (hyph.) 7 16 187 111 150 171 100 173 66 142 85

P County off the NE tip of Scotland (2 wds.) 12 51 76 17 83 127 186 92 120 134 27 165 156

Q Tartlike pastry 133 167 208 219

R Understood thoroughly 143 170 157 20 164 199 108 1

S Disparity 158 74 213 21 94 64 183 46 61

T Swinging, cool, copacetic 196 40 162 47 22 93

U Artless, ingenuous 9 95 144 139 26

V Otalgia 214 91 29 181 42 190 25

W "Fair sir, you spat on me on ___ last," says Shylock ("Merchant of Venice") 62 30 148 89 23 221 132 205 6

X Milesian philosopher (c. 640–546? B.C.) 50 115 43 154 77 207

Y Extended 220 129 65 80 69 161 33 209 180 152 204 15

Z Cut slightly 195 54 163 135

Z₁ Spark; trace 67 28 179 101 114 194 18 109 37

No. 57

CLUES

WORDS

A. Pine away; brood over misfortune (4 wds.) . . . . . `22` `199` `152` `100` `168` `49` `190` `35` `121` `1` `69` `42` `82` `7` `149`

B. Drunkard. . . . . `99` `65` `113`

C. Fielding novel (2 wds.) . . `170` `6` `101` `143` `83` `167` `64`

D. Laugh boisterously (hyph.) . `13` `110` `164` `182` `117` `188`

E. Tragedy (458 B.C.) by Aeschylus . . . . `72` `187` `95` `14` `193` `86` `31` `36` `18`

F. Sartre play that opened in N.Y. in 1948 (2 wds. after *The*) . . . . `33` `9` `80` `40` `150` `174` `177` `185` `93` `197` `45` `112` `57` `11` `127` `118` `192` `2` `165`

G. Woven fabric or garment . . `142` `155` `173` `181`

H. Regulate, settle . . . . . `75` `133` `186` `63` `125` `119`

I. Discard. . . . . `166` `129` `184` `161` `200` `34`

J. Brownish-yellow toad of western Europe . . . . . `30` `17` `141` `12` `163` `180` `136` `10` `147` `21`

K. Easy death or means of inducing one. . . . . . . `132` `135` `109` `120` `124` `79` `50` `53` `195` `189`

L. Disturbance, to-do . . . . . `116` `26` `73` `85` `61` `158`

M. "A noble mind disdains ——. / And let his foes triumph in his overthrow") (4 wds.; Greene, "Alphonso, King of Aragon") . . . . `71` `123` `160` `106` `131` `201` `139` `154` `41` `191` `67` `47` `88`

N. Sweetmeat, originally Turkish. . . . . `151` `92` `198` `156` `38` `43`

O. Satisfactory possession or use of anything; pleasure. . `37` `107` `62` `16` `98` `3` `179` `87` `24`

P. Daintily or quaintly pleasing. . . . . `91` `29` `74` `172`

Q. Nickname for infielder Rogers Hornsby . . . . . `48` `148` `134` `176` `171`

R. Prehistoric; very old . . . . `54` `104` `4` `194` `78` `140` `128`

S. Blackthorn. . . . . `8` `145` `70` `44`

T. Prostitute . . . . `175` `52` `137` `178`

U. Imagine. . . . . `20` `146` `115` `105` `56` `102`

V. Small, sharp-beaked bird that creeps on trees. . . . `111` `28` `81` `153` `159` `122` `5`

W. Old Fr. dance in moderately quick quadruple meter . . . `76` `94` `39` `169` `126` `138` `32`

X. Thorough in the performance of duty . . . . . . `59` `77` `96` `19` `114` `90` `144` `51`

Y. Dismiss; turn out . . . . . `157` `60` `183` `15` `97`

Z. Expressionist drama (1920) by Eugene O'Neill (2 wds. after *The*) . . . . . . `130` `66` `23` `46` `55` `58` `162` `25` `89` `196` `84` `108`

Grid

	1 F	2 F	3 O	4 R		5 V	6 C	7 A	8 S	9 F
10 J	11 F	12 J	13 D	14 E		15 Y	16 O	17 J	18 E
19 X	20 U	21 J	22 A	23 Z	24 O	25 Z	26 L	27 C
28 V	29 P	30 J	31 E	32 W	33 F	34 I	35 A	36 E
37 O	38 N	39 W	40 F	41 M	42 A	43 N	44 S	45 F	46 Z
47 M	48 Q	49 A	50 K	51 X	52 T	53 K	54 R	55 R	56 U
57 F	58 Z	59 X	60 Y	61 L	62 O	63 H	64 C	65 B
66 Z	67 M	68 F	69 A	70 S	71 M	72 E	73 L	74 P	75 H
76 W	77 X	78 R	79 K	80 F	81 V	82 A	83 C	84 Z	85 L
86 E	87 O	88 M	89 Z	90 X	91 P	92 N	93 F	94 W	95 E
96 X	97 Y	98 O	99 B	100 A	101 C	102 U	103 V	104 R	105 U	106 M
107 O	108 Z	109 K	110 D	111 V	112 F	113 B	114 X	115 U	116 L
117 D	118 F	119 H	120 K	121 A	122 V	123 M	124 R	125 M
126 W	127 F	128 R	129 I	130 Z	131 M	132 K	133 H	134 Q
135 K	136 J	137 T	138 W	139 M	140 R	141 J	142 G	143 C	144 X
145 S	146 U	147 J	148 Q	149 A	150 F	151 N	152 A	153 V	154 M
155 G	156 N	157 Y	158 L	159 V	160 M	161 I	162 Z	163 J	164 D
165 F	166 I	167 C	168 A	169 W	170 C	171 Q	172 P	173 G	174 F
175 T	176 Q	177 F	178 T	179 O	180 J	181 G	182 D	183 Y
184 I	185 F	186 H	187 E	188 D	189 K	190 A	191 M	192 F	193 E
194 R	195 K	196 Z	197 F	198 N	199 A	200 I	201 M

No. 58

CLUES / WORDS

A Wife of the Duke of Albany ("King Lear") — 161 122 201 153 107 37 117

B Group of poems (1930) by T.S. Eliot (2 wds.) — 196 108 114 69 192 141 133 67 149 177 194 58

C "Heavies" — 48 131 33 6 103 199 87 26

D One of a set of chemically identical species of atom which have the same atomic number but different mass numbers — 23 81 63 112 187 98 12

E Good-for-nothing (hyph.) —

F A people of SW Nigeria — 159 116 102 189 61 132 45 203 32 144

G Fine muslin — 157 55 79 5 16 60

H Containing all recent facts, statistics, etc. (3 wds.) — 15 111 134 47 73 13 28

I Hurtful; guilty — 135 173 89 99 198 110 186 34

J Some stones — 119 179 129 106 148 92

K Unseemly display of feelings — 39 72 11 138

L "... The handle toward my hand? Come, ____," says Macbeth (4 wds.) — 125 22 164 38 42

M Sharp; alert; with it (3 wds.) — 95 10 130 163 49 18 150 197 180 29 41 121 59 183 17

N Pleasing artifices — 143 35 82 171 200 43 156 7 57

O Encore! Twice — 166 158 137 80 182

P Bested in battle — 178 147 66

Q Prodigious; magnificent — 70 25 78 100 83 128 36 51 1

R Rough-and-ready; he-man (hyph.) — 162 50 115 174 44 185 77

S Open fabric used in upholstery, theatrical curtains, etc. — 14 113 24 101 75 170 62 9 142

T Affects with a strong tingle of emotion — 21 53 86 118 97

U Timely — 68 146 64 88 27 155 165

V Boo-boos; lemons — 19 154 188 93 127 74 85 195 3

W Harnessed (2 wds.) — 71 136 167 20 152 124 193 8

X Conflict between rival organizations that is kept secret from outsiders — 169 151 40 202 2 190 123 96 145

Y Traditional title of Rembrandt's most famous group painting (2 wds. after *The*) — 172 140 191 65 120 54 104 90 176 4

Z Curse, execration — 139 56 175 126 30 184 76 94

No. 59

CLUES

A. Claymore, e.g. 166 46 162 133 75 29 124 155 64 86

B. Showy; lavish 187 173 16 13 73 147 111

C. "Christ was a carpenter / And not a ___ servant" (Blake, "On Arts and Artists") 156 16 65 96 127 140 28

D. Buffalo Bob Smith's TV sidekick (2 wds.) 18 82 175 184 80 47 177 113 72 183

E. Spill the beans (2 wds.) 7 134 169 37 39 48

F. Author of two of the Epistles . . 106 19 128 53 79

G. Type of break 21 85 159 57 66 172 51 11

H. Macduff (3 wds., "Macbeth") . . 179 121 45 24 105 33 5 114 56 181 78

I. Home 149 130 117 132 102 88

J. Harmonious motion or proportion 157 163 116 110 60 25 92 30 171

K. Hideaway 164 146 101 168

L. Happen as a result of natural growth 36 109 148 20 12 97

M. Mass. birthplace of Nathaniel Hawthorne 135 107 104 23 182

N. River, N England, flowing to the North Sea 144 95 63 189

O. Bounders 6 143 14 61

P. She had to wear the scarlet letter (first name) 129 27 10 17 15 94

Q. Entrancing 32 158 186 150 112 142 160 81 115

R. Whole 41 74 188 55 35 131

S. Scatter 154 141 9 125 62

T. Anc. Gr. personification of death 91 44 43 71 1 120 31 42

U. Knead 145 136 119 153 49 2 76

V. One of Robin Hood's Merry Men (hyph.) 59 100 170 174 40 152 165 84 68 122

W. Type of bucket; abandon; destroy 38 161 178 138 87 67 99

X. Apace 69 58 185 137 103 22 123

Y. Execrable 52 70 108 89 54 8 4

Z. Calif. herb, genus Orthocarpus (hyph.) 3 151 26 118 34 176 180 77 139 50

Z₁. Crowded tenement 83 167 98 126 93 90

WORDS

(Grid — letters with clue assignments)

9 S	10 P	11 G	1 T	2 U	3 Z	4 Y	5 H		6 O
19 F	20 L	21 G		12 L	13 B	14 O	15 P	16 C	17 P
30 J	31 T	32 Q	33 H	34 Z	35 R	36 L	37 E	38 W	39 E
40 V	41 R	42 T	43 T	44 T	45 H	46 A	47 D		48 E
49 U	50 Z		51 G	52 Y	53 F	54 Y	55 H	56 H	57 G
58 X	59 V	60 J	61 O	62 S	63 N	64 A	65 C	66 G	67 W
68 V	69 X	70 Y	71 T	72 D	73 B	74 R	75 A	76 U	
77 Z	78 H	79 F	80 D	81 Q	82 D	83 Z₁	84 V	85 G	86 A
87 W	88 I	89 Y	90 Z₁	91 T	92 J	93 Z₁	94 P	95 N	
96 C	97 L	98 Z₁	99 W	100 V	101 K	102 I	103 X	104 M	105 H
106 F	107 M	108 Y	109 L	110 J	111 B	112 B	113 D	114 H	115 Q
116 J	117 I	118 Z	119 U	120 T	121 H	122 V	123 X	124 A	125 S
126 Z₁	127 C	128 F	129 P	130 I	131 R	132 I	133 A	134 E	135 M
136 U	137 X	138 W	139 Z	140 C	141 S	142 Q	143 O	144 N	
145 U	146 K	147 B	148 L	149 I	150 Q	151 Z	152 V	153 U	
154 S	155 A	156 C	157 J	158 Q	159 G	160 Q	161 W	162 A	
163 J	164 K	165 V	166 A	167 Z₁	168 K	169 E	170 V	171 J	172 G
173 B	174 V	175 D	176 Z	177 D	178 W	179 H	180 Z	181 H	
182 M	183 D	184 D	185 X	186 Q	187 B	188 R	189 N		

No. 60

CLUES

A Creature slain by the beamish boy's vorpal blade ("Through the Looking-Glass"). — 160 135 41 84 146 21 193 178 81 157

B Pertaining to smelling. — 86 98 120 124 47 14 108 10 29

C Sanctifies. — 82 100 155 180 33 60 22

D Very prudish (hyph.). — 191 184 137 43 92 129 149 62 97

E Drool. — 89 75 40 26 163 17

F O.T. prophet. — 76 36 150 153 159 183

G Daughters of Zeus and Mnemosyne. — 32 80 85 186 96

H Yield. — 5 13 119 53 46 74

I Void. — 167 73 39 145 189 19 71

J Am. theologian and metaphysician (1703–58; "The Freedom of the Will"). — 143 94 134 9 65 115 190

K Pa. artists' colony on the Delaware River (2 wds.). — 170 103 182 128 66 142 158

L Gleam, flash; strike obliquely. — 152 8 105 114 141 91

M Short, descriptive word or phrase. — 38 118 130 177 102

N Not permitted or authorized. — 95 70 117 156 90 187 28

O Haunt; specter; scare. — 154 110 35 83 162

P Great Giant pitcher, 1928–43. — 48 165 69 175 20 42 99

Q Disease affecting the hock joint of horses. — 106 109 49 77 173 166

R Discerning; fearful. — 113 6 16 55 78 15 111 125 30 61 172 144

S 1925 Milt Gross book "gradually dedicated" to "The guy that invented dumbwaiters and thin walls" (2 wds.). — 132 140 58 88 67 174 23 131

T Blubbers. — 79 72 101 50

U Violent mental agitation; rage. — 116 147 25 151 59 181

V Son of Calliope who was torn apart by maenads. — 179 139 37 148 169 168

W Fabric used for tablecloths, shelf-coverings, etc. — 31 27 87 107 176 54 1 138

X Companies, bands, herds, swarms. — 127 136 122 133 64 44

Y Refuse. — 116 126 171 11 68 34 52 7 123

Z Person not belonging to a particular group (3 wds.). — 161 126 171 11 68 34 52 7 123

Z₁ Sing in a full, rolling voice. — 188 24 121 185 63

Z₂ Goods, property. — 192 164 56 3 51 93 104

CLUES

A. Slang term for piano (hyph.)
B. Not anticipated (2 wds.)
C. Two-handled ancient vase
D. Heavenly, fabulous (4 wds.)
E. Licentious, dissolute man
F. Chimpanzees, gorillas, orangutans, and gibbons (2 wds.)
G. Burrowing, herbivorous marsupials of Australia
H. Long on looks, pretty as a picture (hyph.)
I. Type of paté or sausage
J. Also (2 wds.)
K. A rare-earth element
L. Road-house; cabaret
M. Candor
N. Where "Falconbridge, the young baron of England" bought his behavior, says Portia ("Merchant of Venice")
O. One who prophesies doom
P. Official "grievance man"
Q. Knavery
R. Another name for the red trillium
S. Skillfully, adroitly
T. Olympic decathlon winner, 1960 (full name)
U. One who can be relied upon (hyph.)
V. Drank to
W. What many an authority takes upon installation (3 wds.)
X. Macaque (2 wds.)
Y. "Thousands counted every groan / And ____ made his woe her own" (Arnold, "The Grande Chartreuse")

WORDS

Clue	Numbers
A	222 81 59 208 18 166 178 127 28 88 20
B	92 198 12 21 84 99 51 65 162 102 147
C	191 140 40 192 176
D	5 225 109 79 142 83 204 74 62 64 148 103 217 164
E	31 197 123 76 54 183 67 216
F	113 58 189 133 106 144 15 70 66 156 215 43 120 39
G	211 36 218 85 73 94 108
H	124 210 24 138 160 47 100 188 141 145
I	25 107 187 153 80 34 174 149 119 180
J	196 117 181 33 22 82
K	157 203 87 213 57 61 14
L	53 122 177 38 169 114
M	175 91 184 209 146 75 1
N	19 221 55 93 101 72 163 190 143 182
O	4 17 226 23 52 186 199 32 205
P	224 121 35 3 115 112 152 134 11
Q	161 30 132 104 168 7 185 63 194
R	179 155 50 201 159 223 195 86 60
S	89 37 167 202 49 139 16 172
T	45 165 97 131 220 98 2 105 29 158 193 27
U	42 129 219 128 77 154 171
V	206 137 111 126 207 48 8
W	151 44 170 130 26 90 173 78 41 118 9 214
X	56 95 136 150 6 200 110 10 116 46 212 69
Y	13 71 125 96 135 68

Diagram

1 M	2 T	3 P	■	4 O	5 D	6 X	7 Q	8 V	9 W	
10 X	11 P	12 B	13 Y	14 K	15 F	16 S	17 O	18 A	19 N	20 A
21 B	22 J	23 O	24 H	25 I	■	26 W	27 T	28 A	29 T	30 Q
31 E	32 O	33 J	34 I	■	35 P	36 G	37 S	38 L	39 F	40 C
41 W	42 U	43 F	■	44 W	45 T	46 X	47 H	48 V	49 S	50 R
51 B	52 O	53 L	54 E	55 N	56 X	57 K	58 F	59 A	60 R	61 K
62 D	63 Q	64 D	65 B	66 F	67 E	68 Y	69 X	70 F	71 Y	■
72 N	73 G	74 D	75 M	76 E	77 U	78 W	79 D	80 I	■	■
81 A	82 J	83 D	84 B	85 G	86 R	87 K	88 A	89 S	■	■
90 W	91 M	92 B	93 N	94 G	95 X	96 Y	97 T	98 T	■	■
99 B	100 H	101 N	102 B	103 D	104 Q	105 T	106 F	107 I	108 G	■
109 D	110 X	111 V	112 P	113 F	114 L	115 P	116 X	117 J	118 W	■
119 I	120 F	121 P	122 L	123 E	124 H	125 Y	126 V	127 A	128 U	■
129 U	130 W	131 T	132 Q	133 F	134 P	135 Y	136 X	137 V	138 H	■
139 S	140 C	141 H	142 D	143 N	144 F	145 H	146 M	147 B	■	■
148 D	149 I	150 X	151 W	152 P	153 I	154 U	155 R	156 F	157 K	158 T
159 R	160 H	161 Q	162 B	163 N	164 D	165 T	166 A	167 S	168 Q	■
169 L	170 W	171 U	172 S	173 W	174 I	175 M	176 C	177 L	178 A	■
179 R	180 I	181 J	182 N	183 E	184 M	185 Q	186 O	187 I	188 H	■
189 F	190 N	191 C	192 C	193 T	194 Q	195 R	196 J	197 E	■	■
198 B	199 O	200 X	201 R	202 S	203 K	204 D	205 T	206 V	■	■
207 V	208 A	209 M	210 H	211 G	212 X	213 K	214 W	215 F	216 E	■
217 D	218 G	219 U	220 T	221 N	222 A	223 R	224 P	225 D	226 O	■

No. 62

CLUES

A Saint of the rich tried to stop her

B Old wife Anne, formerly, has a way with her

C Itching toe—last of the bizarre placekicker, maybe (2 wds.)

D Shingles? You might need these (2 wds.)

E Photographer's aid measuring 99 cm.? (2 wds.)

F Horrid deed, spoiled next in lasting longer

G Cheaper horse stumbled, did badly inside

H Low singer-actress who might have been named Minnie

I Small shot to a point in the earth and wept

J Secures Muslims in wastelands

K Feeble little devil to return tattered net

L The capital one's temper

M Dulls bad taste with goddess of youth

N In it, I have a partner to begin with

O Fine, trite display for a queen

P Absolved quiet ramble

Q Four into fifty-one, near Rome

R Disdain of little Georgia, sitting in a strange corner

S Shabbily encases unkempt livery that must be endured (2 wds.)

T Overwhelming destruction of rotten liar

U Rhine's scampering mouse

V Farewell—also dole out love (hyph.)

W Feigned, acted with very loud English accent

X Streamlined shape prorated out

Y Disloyal if a hunt falls out with a bad case of flu

Z Pain in stomach?

WORDS

A 37 158 84 129 77 208 185 10 203 196 93

B 106 11 88 30 38 202 199 144

C 8 128 79 192 67 105 122 183 174 75 178 155

D 50 189 204 110 74 172 210 184 141 103 169 154

E 200 160 26 59 207 91 125 102 148 112

F 182 124 118 214 68 206 56

G 132 213 120 52 86 24 65 108

H 20 92 114 71 119 159 140

I 7 57 170 98 90 164

J 135 49 63 43 121

K 97 146 9 111 167 31 76 58

L 66 70 115 165

M 23 13 142 60 81 54 191 5 177

N 6 166 27 22 101 32 16 95 117

O 55 107 180 171 100 139 45 15 145

P 18 83 12 152 64 131

Q 73 151 130 19 143 33

R 53 181 187 42 205 80 25 162 201

S 161 123 62 216 138 87 193 34 17 3 150 51 69

T 29 136 197 215 85 44 157 163 94 48

U 82 2 40 137 99 149

V 176 156 186 198 39 134 209 211

W 72 41 179 113 126 78 173 195

X 212 109 168 4 133 190 35 147

Y 153 14 188 46 175 1 89 36 194 116

Z 104 127 47 96 21 61

No. 63

	1 E	2 C	3 R	4 H	5 W	6 U	7 C	8 Q	9 V
10 O	11 F	12 E	13 L	14 Z₁	15 Y	16 K	17 G	18 Z₁	19 M	20 V
21 J	22 C	23 V	24 Z	25 Y	26 X	27 Z	28 U	29 S	30 B	
31 H	32 B	33 P	34 X	35 F	36 H	37 X	38 J	39 L		
40 I	41 I	42 Q	43 Z	44 V	45 L	46 X	47 O	48 P	49 B	50 U
51 R	52 Q	53 W	54 F	55 E	56 A	57 N	58 M	59 F	60 Z₁	61 V
62 E	63 L	64 R	65 H	66 C	67 S	68 D	69 E	70 K	71 X	72 J
73 T	74 H	75 Z₁	76 K	77 B	78 H	79 U	80 V	81 O	82 E	
83 T	84 U	85 L	86 D	87 M	88 T	89 V	90 G	91 X	92 B	
93 P	94 A	95 G	96 Z₁	97 M	98 K	99 Z	100 Z₁	101 M	102 J	103 D
104 A	105 N	106 X	107 V	108 T	109 P	110 F	111 C	112 O	113 B	114 W
115 P	116 K	117 U	118 S	119 H	120 C	121 P	122 L	123 U		
124 P	125 O	126 G	127 R	128 S	129 L	130 B	131 W	132 F	133 J	134 A
135 R	136 W	137 B	138 X	139 Y	140 Z	141 Z₁	142 R	143 X	144 R	
145 Q	146 J	147 U	148 T	149 N	150 Z	151 S	152 T	153 J	154 R	155 Y
156 A	157 W	158 T		159 Z	160 P	161 X	162 V	163 D		
164 X	165 P	166 B	167 N	168 J	169 G	170 Z	171 R	172 F	173 D	174 I
175 Z	176 C	177 D	178 C	179 X	180 E	181 B	182 Y	183 I	184 Q	
185 O	186 Z	187 Y	188 N	189 X	190 U	191 E	192 A	193 O	194 G	195 D
196 F	197 T	198 G	199 V	200 Q	201 M	202 N	203 F	204 Z	205 X	
206 W	207 Z	208 B	209 Z₁	210 I	211 G	212 Y	213 Z	214 W		
215 V	216 I	217 R	218 Q	219 G	220 F	221 W	222 N	223 B		

No. 64

The numbered diagram (acrostic grid). Cell contents (number — clue letter):

Cell	Letter	Cell	Letter	Cell	Letter	Cell	Letter
1	Q	52	Q	103	G	154	C
2	J	53	I	104	C	155	V
3	V	54	Y	105	Z	156	S
4	C	55	B	106	R	157	M
5	D	56	G	107	O	158	K
6	A	57	A	108	E	159	W
7	B	58	X	109	X	160	D
8	M	59	L	110	C	161	E
9	Z	60	J	111	O	162	C
10	V	61	Y	112	M	163	W
11	F	62	Z	113	Z	164	N
12	B	63	W	114	Y	165	Y
13	N	64	T	115	Q	166	N
14	E	65	I	116	B	167	F
15	W	66	Z1	117	F	168	D
16	I	67	X	118	K	169	T
17	Z1	68	Y	119	A	170	V
18	L	69	H	120	D	171	J
19	Y	70	Y	121	W	172	C
20	Q	71	M	122	N	173	L
21	C	72	N	123	G	174	G
22	R	73	O	124	H	175	F
23	R	74	L	125	R	176	W
24	A	75	Z	126	U	177	Q
25	Y	76	V	127	U	178	P
26	Q	77	Z1	128	S	179	J
27	H	78	Z	129	X	180	J
28	D	79	S	130	B	181	Y
29	X	80	K	131	C	182	V
30	W	81	A	132	S	183	C
31	L	82	P	133	T	184	T
32	J	83	C	134	W	185	S
33	V	84	Y	135	A	186	Y
34	L	85	U	136	Z	187	E
35	Q	86	G	137	Y	188	E
36	I	87	C	138	K	189	R
37	P	88	W	139	Z1	190	W
38	Y	89	O	140	X	191	I
39	M	90	Q	141	S	192	C
40	D	91	D	142	Z	193	T
41	X	92	P	143	H	194	Q
42	O	93	Z1	144	R	195	Y
43	M	94	O	145	I	196	X
44	J	95	I	146	E	197	J
45	C	96	W	147	Z1	198	D
46	N	97	V	148	W	199	U
47	S	98	Y	149	Q	200	N
48	C	99	F	150	O	201	J
49	Z	100	A	151	A	202	R
50	Z1	101	T	152	U	203	F
51	R	102	S	153	M	204	C

CLUES

A. Heavenly, airy 24 81 151 6 100 57 135 119

B. Pleated frilling 7 55 130 12 116

C. 1937 song from the film "The Hurricane" (3 wds.) 48 21 154 83 172 87 204 4 162 110 131 183 192 104 45

D. Object or result desired or sought after 120 5 198 28 40 168 160 91

E. Work one's way through the earth 146 14 161 187 108 188

F. Formation of the egg and its preparation for fertilization and development 175 203 117 99 11 167

G. Recurring theme in an artistic work 56 174 123 103 86

H. Flock of larks or quails 69 143 27 124

I. Intent, serious 16 95 65 53 36 145 191

J. Mutiny leader ("Mutiny on the Bounty") 180 2 201 60 44 171 179 197 32

K. King of England, Norway, and Denmark (995?-1035) 158 138 118 80

L. Labor leader (1880-1969), founder of the CIO 173 74 59 18 34

M. Gives (oneself) over, as to a habit or pursuit; those who are so given over 43 71 112 8 39 153 157

N. Species of plantain with long, narrow leaves 166 122 72 46 13 200 164

O. Another name for a hero sandwich 150 94 107 111 42 89 73

P. Richly embroidered, apron-like vestment worn by the high priest (Judaism) 82 37 178 31 92

Q. Got the better of by scheming (2 wds.) 26 90 177 194 115 20 35 52 149 1

R. Summons to appear in court; reference to an authority or a precedent 51 125 106 189 23 144 202 22

S. Navel; central point 79 132 102 185 156 128 47 141

T. Seaport at the mouth of the Loire, W France 169 133 184 193 64 101

U. Camels, in India 85 199 126 152 127

V. Temper, lessen the severity of 97 182 76 33 170 10 155 3

W. Velvet grass (2 wds.) 190 148 121 176 15 63 30 96 88 159 163 134

X. Cheats 29 67 129 109 58 196 41 140

Y. Principally, primarily (4 wds.) 38 68 165 181 186 19 137 114 54 61 98 25 70 84 195

Z. Father of John the Baptist (Luke 1:5) 136 105 9 62 75 78 113 49 142

Z₁. 1872 satirical novel by Samuel Butler 93 147 139 17 77 66 50

WORDS

No. 65

CLUES

A Extra time, space, etc. within which to operate . . . .
66 77 4 12 22 130

B 1883 song written by Princess Regent Liliuokalani (2 wds.) . .
73 173 131 47 125 79 202

C List, register . . . .
56 111 154 163 67 172

D Extreme satisfaction . . . .
122 150 28 2 180 35 95

E Hindu expression on meeting or parting . . . .
185 121 97 135 178 153 143

F Part of the coast of Antarctica, discovered in 1831 (2 wds.) . . .
116 88 186 82 201 37 30 21 9 78 189

G Without delay (2 wds.) . . . . . .
197 190 124 134 92 53 3 51

H Aspiring; pretentious . . . .
145 118 149 69 68 177 45 152 161

I London prison torn down in 1902 . . . .
85 120 86 33 60 65 36

J Appalling . . . .
113 104 26 155 192 194 81 75

K Abase oneself . . . .
43 63 133 19 141 49

L Give confidence . . . .
167 39 146 132 72 57

M Inappropriate . . . .
160 64 6 18 50 61 184 142 90 183

N Very weak . . . .
170 158 13 151 1 42

O Halves . . . .
10 171 174 198 129 5 117 191

P "The Fox and the Grapes," "The Tortoise and the Hare," etc. (2 wds.)
89 200 99 48 20 166 193 179 17 157 11 139

Q "____, and now's the hour" (3 wds.; Burns, "Scots, Wha Hae")
32 188 46 115 103 144 59 112 7 23

R Major prophet of the 6th and 7th centuries B.C. . . . .
159 169 25 110 105 96 29 164

S In complete disorder (2 wds.) . .
54 27 107 87 62 24 119 80 71 195

T From dusk till dawn . . . .
127 31 8 109 140 147 156 101 165

U Increase in intensity, magnitude, etc. . . . .
16 128 83 181 138 136 94

V "Where more is meant than ____" (3 wds.; Milton, "Il Penseroso") . . . .
168 38 98 162 114 70 137 176 196 123 15

W Unconventional . . . .
148 199 175 58 106 84 34

X Haggis ingredient . . . .
100 14 108 182 203 55 76

Y "There is no ____ under the sun" (2 wds., Eccl. 1:8) . . . . . .
74 102 41 40 93 126 44 187

---

1 N	2 D	3 G	4 A	5 O	6	7 Q	8 T
9 F	10 O	11 P	12 A	13 N	14 X	15 V	
18 M	19 K	20 P	21 F	22 A	23 Q	24 S	25 R	26 J	27 S
28 D	29 R	30 F	31 T	32 Q	33	34 W	35 D	36 I	37 F
38 V	39 L	40 Y	41 Y	42 N	43 K	44 Y	45 H	46 Q	
47 B	48 P	49 K	50 M	51 G	52 J	53 G	54 S	55 X
56 C	57 L	58 W	59 Q	60 I	61 M	62 S	63 K	64 M	65 I
66 A	67 C	68 H	69 H	70 V	71 S	72 L	73 B	74 Y
75 J	76 X	77 A	78 F	79 B	80 S	81 J	82 F	83 U
84 W	85 I	86 I	87 S	88 F	89 P	90 M	91 U	92 G
93 Y	94 U	95 D	96 R	97 E	98 V	99 P	100 X	101 T	102 Y
103 Q	104 J	105 R	106 W	107 S	108 X	109 T	110 R	111 C	112 Q
113 J	114 V	115 Q	116 F	117 O	118 H	119 S	120 I	121 E	122 D
123 V	124 G	125 B	126 Y	127 T	128 U	129 O	130 A	131 B	132 N
133 K	134 G	135 E	136 U	137 V	138 U	139 P	140 T	141 K	
142 M	143 E	144 Q	145 H	146 L	147 T	148 W	149 H		
150 D	151 N	152 H	153 E	154 C	155 J	156 T	157 P	158 N	
159 R	160 M	161 H	162 V	163 C	164 R	165 T	166 P	167 L	168 V
169 R	170 N	171 O	172 C	173 B	174 O	175 W	176 V	177 H	
178 E	179 P	180 D	181 U	182 X	183 M	184 M	185 E	186 F	
187 Y	188 Q	189 F	190 G	191 O	192 J	193 P	194 J		
195 S	196 V	197 G	198 O	199 W	200 P	201 F	202 B	203 X	

CLUES

A. Am. novelist (1876–1916; "Martin Eden"; full name). — 92 140 55 36 160 151 166 15 207 214

B. What bats use to establish their position (2 wds.) — 104 150 115 37 161 19 164 177 206 119 122 60

C. Scorpion, e.g. — 7 26 46 35 19 108 4 17

D. Brit. term for a donkey. — 29 211 11 59 168

E. Composition made up of bits of other works. — 30 137 54 127 96 45 169 194

F. Gradual interpenetration. — 44 198 208 50 136 95 142 88 103 179 28 178

G. Give courage to — 87 191 91 24 23 53 116 102

H. Compassion, pity — 68 78 156 74

I. Rare; choice; obscure — 3 165 145 205 192 82 13 70 63

J. Ill-will — 172 158 1 107 72 76

K. Overwhelming influx — 148 66 159 22 124 105 94 201 75

L. Not developed, accomplished, or realized. — 25 98 184 38 58 123 34 212 120 42 106

M. Roman general and consul, opponent of Sulla (c. 155–86 B.C.). — 41 170 135 14 203 27

N. Declaim — 101 86 213 18 67

O. "Alas! Why gnaw you so your ___?" (2 wds.; "Othello"). — 132 16 188 84 163 49 153 10 77

P. Stingy (hyph.). — 113 134 62 118 79 80 157 187 114 51 139

Q. He became president of Egypt in 1970. — 182 6 9 112 64

R. Laying open to view — 152 138 141 97 129 215 185 125 133

S. Chronicle. — 8 71 210 186 190 126 171 93

T. Mainstay (2 wds.). — 196 52 100 183 65 33 147 21 155

U. The art of swimming — 149 131 89 2 73 209 202 47

V. Australian and New Zealand soldiers of WW I — 121 130 204 85 12 180 173

W. Sidetrack. — 5 195 57 144 200

X. Sword handles, e.g. — 111 128 48 32 99

Y. Harmony. — 40 20 175 56 39 197

Z. Extended shortage; lack of rain — 162 43 81 174 109 146 61

Z₁. West — 90 167 117 181 154 143 189 69

Z₂. Scottish engineer and inventor (1736–1819). — 193 31 83 199

WORDS

No. 67

CLUES

		WORDS
A	Literal legal interpretation (4 wds.)	218 50 99 206 165 88 11 23 170 105 2 57 75 36
B	Of the nature of alms	5 174 13 37 74 9 205 83 102 45 225 219
C	Continuously, without a break (4 wds.)	184 162 32 41 138 168 193 91 171 204 224 117
D	Within the hull of a ship	101 7 93 153 186 157 58
E	Of sound	89 127 140 56 139
F	Stands on high	104 96 49 90 18 197
G	Alert; quickly perceptive (hyph.)	185 43 22 161 14 107 192
H	Highly irritating or annoying	119 69 208 200 53 111 212 142 42
I	Errand or purpose for which one is sent	216 34 59 137 47 106 40
J	Wealth, abundance	52 126 8 211 176 134 76 194 199
K	Apt	202 62 6 133 39 54 210 98
L	Eager to enjoy; lustful	173 195 63 103 143 131 215 183 122
M	Coming	147 163 114 21 28 223
N	Fungi of the genus Tuber	123 116 136 152 221 180 87 191
O	Muse of music and lyric poetry	85 222 82 113 190 17 141
P	City on the Loire, central France	12 155 181 146 71 68
Q	Meddle	160 92 110 196 61 95 25 4 115
R	Launcelot's surname ("The Merchant of Venice")	108 158 124 150 78
S	Lingered; brooded over	100 175 86 81 97 125 166
T	Moved with short, light steps	30 154 172 217 44 179 201
U	Cars on rails for carrying loads in a mine	48 16 27 203 77
V	Secret (hyph.)	31 73 178 109 118 189 20 145
W	Elude or get the better of by adroitness	207 120 60 135 3 198 129 55 159 151 177
X	Endured	15 84 149 67 10 164 182 112 24
Y	Modern exhortation to try (3 wds.)	121 188 35 167 66 80 46
Z	Nymph of the Mohammedan paradise; voluptuously alluring	72 169 65 33 132
Z₁	Gigantic three-horned Cretaceous dinosaur	64 128 19 51 226 148 220 187 29 156 214
Z₂	Vain cause of terror	213 79 209 26 94 38 144 70 1

1 Z₂	2 A	3 W	4 Q	5 B		6 K	7 D	8 J	9 B
10 X	11 A	12 P	13 B		14 G	15 X	16 U	17 O	18 F	19 Z₁
20 Q	21 M	22 G	23 A	24 X	25 Q	26 Z₂	27 U	28 M	29 H	
30 T	31 V	32 C	33 Z	34 I	35 Y	36 A	37 B	38 Z₂		
39 K	40 I	41 C	42 H	43 G	44 T	45 B	46 Y	47 I		
48 U	49 F	50 A	51 Z₁	52 J	53 H	54 K	55 W	56 E		
57 A	58 D	59 I	60 W	61 Q	62 K	63 L	64 Z₁	65 Z	66 Y	67 X
68 P	69 H	70 Z₂	71 P	72 Z	73 V	74 B	75 A	76 J		
77 U	78 R	79 Z₂	80 Y	81 S	82 O	83 B	84 X	85 O	86 S	87 N
88 A	89 E	90 F	91 C	92 Q	93 D	94 Z₂	95 Q	96 Q	97 S	
98 K	99 A	100 S	101 D	102 B	103 L	104 F	105 A	106 I	107 G	
108 R	109 V	110 Q	111 H	112 X	113 O	114 M	115 Q	116 N	117 C	
118 V	119 H	120 W	121 Y	122 L	123 N	124 R	125 S	126 J	127 E	128 Z₁
129 W	130 C	131 L	132 Z	133 K	134 J		135 W	136 N	137 I	138 C
139 E	140 E	141 O	142 H	143 L	144 Z₂	145 V	146 P	147 M	148 Z₁	
149 X	150 R	151 W	152 N	153 D	154 T	155 P	156 Z₁	157 D	158 R	
159 W	160 Q	161 G	162 C	163 M	164 X	165 A	166 S	167 Y		
168 C	169 Z	170 A	171 C	172 T	173 L	174 B	175 S	176 J	177 W	
178 V	179 T	180 N	181 P	182 X	183 L	184 C	185 G	186 D	187 Z₁	
188 Y	189 V	190 O	191 N	192 G	193 C	194 J	195 L	196 Q	197 F	
198 W	199 J	200 H	201 T	202 K	203 U	204 C	205 B	206 A	207 W	
208 H	209 Z₂	210 K	211 J	212 H	213 Z₂	214 Z₁	215 L	216 I		
217 T	218 A	219 B	220 Z₁	221 N	222 O	223 M	224 C	225 B	226 Z₁	

No. 68

CLUES

A Edify 79 144 72 43 42 162 17 129 106

B Daunted, discomposed 64 76 131 36 159

C Final result 136 22 90 122 100 13

D Large power-driven boat 94 113 24 28 3 119

E Shropshire town often mentioned by Housman 110 68 147 93 126 83

F Elevated; distinguished 154 63 137 143 35 53 9 107

G Mohammedan month of fasting by day 46 87 39 152 82 33 60

H "Contempt, farewell! and maiden pride, adieu! / No glory lives behind ___ of such" (2 wds., "Much Ado") 71 155 56 74 92 161 98

I Due, imputable (to) 38 62 12 169 52

J Instrument of torture; extreme pain 150 18 45 78

K Fr. dramatic poet (1639-99; "Andromaque", "Athalie") 132 48 37 112 70 146

L Confederate general (1817-72); leader of Lee's advance at Gettysburg 81 124 164 58 115

M Wild mulberry 127 171 121 55 66 104 118

N Off-color 75 163 34 67 10 31

O County in Leinster, Republic of Ireland 97 170 148 29 142 95

P Latin poet (43 B.C.-A.D.18; "Metamorphoses") 61 165 109 15

Q Spanish-born Roman emperor (c. 53-117) 7 101 160 125 120 25

R Charon's river 103 80 54 88

S Article belonging to an incomplete set 116 138 141 153 14 51 85

T Charming, delightful 151 156 19 77 157 5 11 145

U "In nature there's no blemish but ___" (2 wds., "Twelfth Night") 96 86 69 30 89 41 26

V Salad root 65 158 167 84 21 139

W Gravy; found fortune (2 wds.) 130 2 91 173 114 102 44 20 99

X 1925 Irving Berlin hit 105 111 32 140 73 49

Y Nonsensical song by Bert Kalmar and Harry Ruby (4 wds.) 16 8 135 108 172 47 123 117 149 27 166

Z African animal related to the giraffe 23 4 133 134 168

Z_1 Nine iron 6 50 1 57 40 128 59

Grid

1 Z_1	2 W	3 D	4 Z	5 T	6 Z_1					
7 Q	8 Y	9 F	10 N	11 T	12 I	13 C	14 S	15 P		
16 Y	17 A	18 J	19 T	20 W	21 V	22 C	23 Z	24 D	25 Q	26 U
27 Y	28 D	29 O	30 U	31 N	32 X	33 G	34 N	35 F		
36 B	37 K	38 I	39 G	40 Z_1	41 U	42 A	43 A	44 W	45 J	46 G
47 Y	48 K	49 X	50 Z_1	51 S	52 I	53 F	54 R	55 M	56 H	57 Z_1
58 L	59 Z_1	60 G	61 P	62 I	63 F	64 B	65 V	66 M	67 N	
68 E	69 U	70 K	71 H	72 A	73 X	74 H	75 N	76 B	77 T	78 J
79 A	80 R	81 L	82 G	83 E	84 V	85 S	86 U	87 G	88 R	
89 U	90 C	91 W	92 H	93 E	94 D	95 O	96 U	97 O	98 H	
99 W	100 C	101 Q	102 W	103 R	104 M	105 X	106 A	107 F		
108 Y	109 P	110 E	111 X	112 K	113 D	114 W	115 L	116 S	117 Y	118 M
119 D	120 Q	121 M	122 C	123 Y	124 L	125 Q	126 E	127 M	128 Z_1	
129 A	130 W	131 B	132 K	133 Z	134 Z	135 Y	136 C	137 F	138 S	
139 V	140 X	141 S	142 O	143 F	144 A	145 T	146 K	147 E		
148 O	149 Y	150 J	151 T	152 G	153 S	154 F	155 H	156 T		
157 T	158 V	159 B	160 Q	161 H	162 A	163 N	164 L	165 P	166 Y	167 V
168 Z	169 I	170 O	171 M	172 Y	173 W					

No. 69

CLUES

A Out-and-out, complete (hyph.) . . . .

B Members of La Mano Nera, e.g.

C 1759 novel by Voltaire . . . .

D Pin or wedge for fastening and tightening . . . .

E Pressing . . . .

F Eng. author and natural scientist (1834–1913); "Ants, Bees, and Wasps") . . . .

G Piercing . . . .

H AA, to a film star . . . .

I Part of Jotunheim ruled by Skrymir (Scand. myth.) . . . .

J Eng. leader in the Gunpowder plot (1570–1606; full name) . . . .

K Tolkien creations . . . .

L Alarm bell . . . .

M Pawns; hamstrings . . . .

N "Till _____ stand presently at God's great Judgment Seat" (3 wds.; Kipling, "Ballad of East and West") . .

O Pledge; something thrown down as a challenge . . . .

P Disturbance . . . .

Q Play by Goethe . . . .

R World champion chess player, 1927–35, 1937–46 . . . .

S Anglo-Indian luncheon . . . .

T Jessica Tandy role in "Streetcar Named Desire" . . . .

U Brightness . . . .

V Old-time moniker for a Senufo's country (2 wds.) . . . .

W Patient horse . . . .

X Presents . . . .

Y Attractive (4 wds.) . . . .

WORDS

A 36 85 76 111 164 45 10 62 67 97 125 173 50

B 94 28 33 6 181 150 2 42

C 155 127 110 78 88 144 171

D 124 27 168 21 133 92

E 44 141 60 83 15 119

F 79 153 178 65 93 172 5

G 30 157 106 148 7 4 16

H 49 64 145 9 26

I 20 86 41 131 116 72

J 100 136 47 1 160 174 149 81 121

K 163 129 175 43 105 118 56

L 135 180 126 159 113 8

M 146 179 103 138 95

N 120 12 154 122 104 3 46 77 167 132 177

O 165 115 37 61

P 34 40 58 75 69 108

Q 143 90 101 19 161 73

R 59 170 107 29 23 52 99 66

S 158 57 140 91 54 151

T 25 130 102 89 137 166 80

U 84 14 162 98 63 32 128 117

V 142 82 176 11 169 112 156 17 48 53

W 51 123 18 39 35 134

X 114 147 152 22 70

Y 96 109 182 31 74 68 55 87 38 71 139 24 13

7 G	8	L 9	H 10	A 11	V 12	1	J 2	B 3	N 4	G 5	F 6 B
17 V	18	W 19	Q 20	I 21	D		13	Y 14	U 15	E 16 G
27 D	28 B	29	R 30	G 31	Y 32	D	22	X 23	R 24	Y 25	T 26 H
38 Y		V 49	H 50	A 51	W	52	R 53	V	54	S 55	Y 56 K
48 V	39	W 40	P 41	I 42	B		43	K 44	A 46	N 47	J
57 S	58	P 59	R 60	E 61		62	A 63	U 64	H	65	F
66 R	67	A 68	Y	69			71 X	Y 72	I	73	Q 74	Y
75 P	76	A 77	N 78	C 79	F 80	T	81	J 82	V 83	E 84	U 85 A
86 I	87	Y 88	C 89	T 90	Q	91	S 92	D 93	F 94	B 95	M
96 Y	97	A 98	U 99	R 100	J	101	Q 102	T 103	M 104	N 105	K 106 G
107 R	108	P 109	Y 110	C 111	A	112	V 113	L 114	X 115	O 116	I
117 U	118	K 119	E 120	N 121	J	122	N 123	W	124	D 125	A 126 L
127 C		128	U 129	K 130	T 131	I	132	N 133	D 134	W 135	L 136 J
137 T	138	M 139	Y	140	S 141	E 142	N 143	Q 144	C 145	H 146 M
147 X	148	G 149	J 150	B 151	S	152	X 153	F 154	N 155	C 156 V
157 G	158	S 159	L	160	J 161	Q 162	U 163	K 164	A 165	O 166 T
167 N	168	D 169	V 170	R 171	C	172	F 173	A 174	J 175	K 176 V
177 N		178	F 179	M 180	L 181	B 182	Y			
	I									

CLUES

WORDS

A Secluded; unsubstantial 16 162 110 47 6 131 24

B Traditionally, the northern tip of Scotland (4 wds.) 55 122 135 34 204 27 105 12 194 138 186 177 223 198 5 231

C Eng. novelist and poet (1872-1963; "A Glastonbury Romance") . . . 39 213 41 67 51

D Primary; simple; basic 143 19 178 109 169 46 219 101 92 98

E Tenacious; having a good memory 174 45 234 140 70 29 151 148 192

F "The bridal of ———" (3 wds.; George Herbert, "Virtue") . . . 95 66 137 228 196 189 125 222 114 127 87

G Co-winner, 1936 Nobel Prize in physiology and medicine . . 205 129 136 2 1

H Soviet dancer and choreographer, b. 1906 . . . . . 214 147 76 60 33 11 201 97

I Fur of young lambs, with lustrous, closely curled wool . . 15 36 203 142 3 57 230 225 208

J Imbecile, fool 89 144 182 65 183 50

K Female rabbit 111 69 104

L Use of threats to influence someone 38 128 152 157 53 79 200 181 187 107 173 62

M From gunnel to gunnel 86 134 139 150 211 59 179 40 72 227 94 48

N Eng. archaeologist and anthropologist (1903-72; "Adam's Ancestors") 146 233 84 44 133 22

O Scot. expression of incredulity, annoyance, etc. 28 52 124 68

P Flatter in a servile way 224 117 85 217

Q Am. hero of the 1936 Olympic Games 116 188 43 25 218

R Answer 171 42 184 56 88 232 35 100 166

S Bathsheba's husband, e.g. . . . 75 26 161 74 61 126 236

T 1894 novel by George Moore (2 wds.) 58 195 235 132 90 10 78 18 191 163 158 83

U Gr. poet (fl. 648 B.C.) noted for satirical iambic verses . . . 221 164 14 37 170 21 165 115 121 185 175

V Turkish liqueurs 202 113 226 82 119

W Title of the last chapter of Carlyle's "The French Revolution" (4 wds.) 71 153 206 120 212 32 20 13 93 80 102 63 49 172 149 77 180 160 167

X Brothel 112 8 30 96 145 54 159 81 210 118

Y Of the nettle family 23 9 130 193 141 168 64 91 106 156

Z Culture in feelings, taste, manners, etc. 103 31 154 216 229 207 176 215 197 17 4

Z₁ A former name of Australia (2 wds.) 190 220 7 155 209 99 199 73 108 123

No. 71 by Eric N. Compton

CLUES   **WORDS**

A. Clever, humorous remark . . .   160 48 178 191 81 29 129 78 148

B. In a lazy, unoccupied manner . .   54 72 17 62

C. Buddhist holy city, far eastern capital 146 2 168 53 11

D. Type of printing 133 111 1 203 26 56 177 15 135 92 172

E. Demand, require 6 61 123 94 38 22

F. Draw out; cause to be revealed .   14 85 173 33 77 4

G. Compassion, sameness of feeling 80 91 59 25 149 71 208 153

H. "Once more ———" (3 wds., "Henry V") 120 141 196 106 47 19 67 211 102 60 202 112

I. Chewy candy 195 136 98 36 88

J. Having a special, marked flavor .   44 190 55 8 165

K. Tyrannical 159 187 199 164 89 115 110 126 169 3

L. Low point 7 46 117 182 189

M. New England poet (1807-92; "Maud Muller") 49 23 64 104 201 194 167 158

N. Feature of the Normandy countryside, scene of 1944 fighting 10 186 114 184 139 95 83 41 74

O. University town in Pennsylvania .   198 188 205 175 206 35

P. Shot full of holes 109 28 86 147 197 24 87

Q. Opera by Caccini 79 132 13 116 63 210 143 163

R. Prize-winning novel by Herman Wouk (3 wds.) 138 128 156 105 200 73 181 151 152 145 9 97 70 170

S. Chicago settlement founded in 1889 by Jane Addams (2 wds.)   125 76 107 193 166 140 84 185 30

T. Longest river entirely in Spain .   204 171 101 34

U. Kern-Hammerstein song from "Show Boat" (2 wds.) . . .   90 113 150 69 119 39 27 180 154 162 192

V. Unrehearsed, casual 58 66 99 5 93 122 40

W. "Plain" objects on faces 183 108 31 118 57

X. Icelandic epic 100 134 21 50

Y. Industrial city in Ohio 18 144 52 174 75 137 12 32 124 103

Z. 1941 Triple Crown winner 179 45 142 68 16 20 82 42 155

Z₁. Bear the cost of 209 65 207 131 121 96

Z₂. Victory 161 37 127 130 176 43 51

No. 72 by Mary A. Pattison

CLUES

A Attention fixed forever—I've Teddy to thank for it in part · · · 49 38 135 15 158 35 145

B Backward age in a common alternative—all in good season · · · 146 136 117 187 1 124 104

C Home trap, in a way, figuratively speaking · · · 40 68 183 11 176 127 77 55

D In short, note well seven I find will come to a peak in Britain (2 wds.) · · · 90 133 86 182 149 34 154 120

E You'll find Spenser's love poems here if you have at it more agitatedly · · · 186 10 84 37 23 141 106 161

F Could be that UN VIP (2 wds.) · · · 54 112 42 85 155 29

G Wipe out former equivoque, give extremes · · · 144 70 160 8 14 89 31

H This can be heard notedly in blue · · · 63 184 123 41 76 21 116 6

I Depressions for an ice skater? One accosts him to find out · · · 165 96 172 26 91 102 80 17 46 188 74

J Approach sharp headland with keen appetite · · · 81 33 82 108 178 148 185 73 130

K Murderous trio at the card table · · · 168 152 138 66 107 122 132 163 79

L Boat to put up with for sauce · · · 171 69 98 162 67

M Tree mix Ty mixed in great distress · · · 126 193 36 83 51 65 13 114 180

N Company with awful fear to restate claim · · · 153 137 142 119 190 9 93 20

O Following jeweler's opening, Mommy's sis becomes quite carefree · · · 95 140 134 192 179 47

P Often heard but unseen, dramatically · · · 7 62 78 61 196 28 167 75

Q Some you thought were quite the lads · · · 197 128 39 99 32

R The girl shows the effects of Time, so make game of her (2 wds.) · · · 53 164 94 22 177 113 3

S Tidy life could change for good reproduction · · · 5 174 52 57 111 181 25 159

T Bird carries husks of grain a short distance · · · 71 100 92 16 105 166 2 170 27

U Ida succeeded where in France? No, she wrote in England · · · 64 110 4 151 191

V The right oven might come very suddenly · · · 169 59 50 143 88 101 156 139 45

W Sounds as if you might have to stand in line for this floral display (2 wds.) · · · 103 60 147 12 173 18 131 195 44 97

X Muslim seems a little sheepish and is so · · · 194 56 175 157 109

Y Neither sharp nor flat nor acquired · · · 24 43 121 115 129 19 58

Z Old mistress? · · · 125 118 189 150 30 87 48 72

No. 73 by Betsy Curtis

CLUES / WORDS

	Clue	Cell numbers
A	Incitement	48 178 16 190 137 162
B	Illegitimate son of WORD E	142 24 13 55 36 164
C	Fanatical	37 117 10 91 32
D	Trembled	58 146 101 159 76 110
E	Legendary king of Britain (full name)	127 66 75 23 145 52 30 188 60 77 183 141
F	Blockhead	9 107 102 97 120
G	Reconsideration (2 wds.)	4 150 46 89 109 80 29 93 170 59 83 14 54 71
H	Distorted	144 87 153 42 186 123 168
I	Wife of Shaharaim (1 Chron. 8,9)	131 106 50 119 8 177
J	Incite (with "on")	19 148 180
K	Genus of herbs of the buttercup family	15 82 12 133 157 20 94
L	The real facts	85 47 17 95 105 40 167
M	Improves with age	100 132 149 28 158 151 169
N	Refuge from the usual, the annoying, or the difficult	79 111 7 38 86
O	Pertaining to rhythmic heart contraction	65 192 92 2 78 45 31 154
P	Type of tug	182 33 90 72 53 41 69
Q	Mythical fire-bringer	128 64 6 118 99 112 161 56 179 143
R	Conforming to professional standards of conduct	84 96 152 163 125 68 11
S	Face (an embankment) with stone	57 135 26 63 160
T	Move about lightly	172 136 121 176
U	"____ and speech they wrought" (Swinburne, "Atalanta in Calydon")	44 73 185 139 166 147 174 156
V	What you get in a mess hall	35 114 27 43
W	Instrument for measuring r.p.m.	173 81 34 22 124 165 187 39 25 98
X	Rock whose constituent minerals have a more or less foliated arrangement	116 126 18 1 134 62
Y	There	74 181 140 113 155 49 61
Z	Religious choral song	108 103 21 88 138 122
Z₁	Lunch (Brit.)	130 51 171 184 70 191 129
Z₂	"When, at ____, one remembers" (Holmes, "Bunker Hill")	175 3 104 67 189

DIAGRAM

1 X	2 O	3 Z₂	4 G	5 E	6 Q	7 N	8 I			
9 F	10 C	11 R	12 K	13 B	14 G	15 K	16 A	17 L	18 X	
19 J	20 K	21 Z	22 W	23 E	24 B	25 W	26 S	27 V	28 M	
29 G	30 E	31 O	32 C	33 P	34 W	35 V	36 B	37 C		
38 N	39 W	40 L	41 P	42 H	43 V	44 U	45 O	46 G	47 L	
48 A	49 Y	50 I	51 Z₁	52 E	53 P	54 G	55 B	56 Q	57 S	
58 D	59 G	60 E	61 Y	62 X	63 S	64 Q	65 O	66 E	67 Z₂	
68 R	69 P	70 Z₁	71 G	72 P	73 U	74 Y	75 E	76 D		
77 E	78 O	79 N	80 G	81 W	82 K	83 G	84 R	85 L	86 N	
87 H	88 Z	89 G	90 P	91 C	92 O	93 G	94 K	95 L		
96 R	97 F	98 W	99 Q	100 M	101 D	102 F	103 Z	104 Z₂	105 L	
106 I	107 F	108 Z	109 G	110 D	111 N	112 Q	113 Y	114 V		
115 E	116 X	117 C	118 Q	119 I	120 F	121 T	122 Z	123 H		
124 W	125 R	126 X	127 E	128 Q	129 Z₁	130 Z₁	131 I	132 M	133 K	134 X
135 S	136 T	137 A	138 Z	139 U	140 Y	141 E	142 B	143 Q		
144 H	145 E	146 D	147 U	148 J	149 M	150 G	151 M	152 R	153 H	154 O
155 Y	156 U	157 K	158 M	159 D	160 S	161 Q	162 A	163 R	164 B	
165 W	166 U	167 L	168 H	169 M	170 G	171 Z₁	172 T	173 W		
174 U	175 Z₂	176 T	177 I	178 A	179 Q	180 J	181 Y	182 P	183 E	
184 Z₁	185 U	186 H	187 W	188 E	189 Z₂	190 A	191 Z₁	192 O		

No. 74 Gordon N. Pons

CLUES

A Member of an ancient monastic brotherhood
57 62 151 73 38 184

B Snare for diurnal insects (2 wds.)
34 24 50 148 68 155 98 74 44 119 210 190

C Silent screen star (full name)
43 115 29 7 177 139 88 188 205

D Am. inventor (1811-61)
197 111 146 23

E Bizarre
135 6 194 36 204 64 202 126 213 2

F Indian butler
144 164 37 61 176 91 140 191

G Spatial locations
137 109 56 192 59

H Am. Revolutionary officer after whom a N.C. city was originally named
45 86 16 72 67 97 127

I Modern domestic title
129 18 174 143 3 180 138 10 199 106 110 31

J Meddling, intrusiveness
183 103 55 158 96 75 52 175 80 141 211 181

K On the slim side
134 112 118 208 107 195 99 149

L One who affects an extravagant love of art
54 193 169 51 132 1 113

M Native of eastern Greece
71 12 123 203 105 187 170 28 15 157

N Overbearing, arbitrary (hyph.)
172 76 120 79 89 27 87 142 85 206

O Commit, obligate
100 84 154 196 95 121 212

P Leftover, remaining
201 49 81 9 104 92 66 153

Q Final outcome; controversial point
35 69 4 152 42

R Graveyard watch, perhaps (2 wds.)
116 63 166 8 20 185 122 70 198 128

S "Among the ___ Star-scattered on the Grass" (FitzGerald, "The Rubáiyát of Omar Khayyám")
117 65 40 209 26 182

T Excessively fastidious
5 41 171 58 93 150 162 156 77 165 17

U Quality of being light and soft
136 30 133 78 21 13 48 60 168 130 32 114

V Bond between calf and heel (3 wds.)
163 47 178 108 161 189 173 19 102 82 131 200 125 14 167 160

W Take a resolute stand
33 147 159 207 25 179

X Strength of spirit or temperamant
94 22 186 11 124 90

Y Type of anti-knock fluid
83 39 46 145 53

No. 75 by Kirk Dodd

	CLUES	WORDS
A	Rummy with tiles (hyph.)	1 221 166 158 149 145 216 143
B	A.L. hurler, 5-time 20-game winner (full name)	208 132 181 154 205 47 140 163 84
C	Mock sea battle	199 6 57 178 83 126 107 99 29
D	Sheer fabric	63 89 211 87 105 198 17
E	Rapidly changing; extremely complex	170 130 210 108 153 111 177 61 21 187 66 34 45
F	Coarse grass of Europe	40 171 129 20 79 186 206
G	Abominable; extremely wicked	50 203 35 92 3 109 56 72 103
H	Grandstander's forte	12 54 102 191 215 125 180 24 9 156 58
I	Hookah	76 144 19 7 101 160 118 167
J	Well	15 162 26 190 75 207 142
K	Shocking	124 94 22 157 2 100 155 137 139 39
L	Specialist in, or collector of, coins, medals, etc.	194 116 128 214 42 65 182 202 5 55 173
M	Saltpeter, e.g.	209 114 69 222 146 165 36
N	1947 Malcolm Lowry novel (3 wds.)	147 11 59 188 219 38 48 78 113 31 67 176 96 123 86
O	Laborers attendant to a hunting party	133 168 117 148 90 74 201
P	Obloquy	112 195 91 16 197 121 161 30
Q	"___ swept thereby / Like an ominous bird a-wing" (4 wds.; Hardy, "Neutral Tones")	200 164 131 60 189 151 217 138 172 106 52 185 73 44 49 122 175
R	Flexible, supple, limber	184 174 71 10 159 82 46
S	Alma mater to Longfellow and Hawthorne	152 127 220 77 104 37 110
T	An advantage of incorporation (2 wds.)	97 23 150 25 213 43 115 33 51 196 183 53 169 119 136 85
U	Pique, provoke	193 95 98 141 13 14 120 70
V	Highway cop (2 wds.)	41 18 62 93 135 88 192 218 80 179 68 4
W	Thistlelike herb, Carthamus tinctorius	212 27 32 81 134 64 28 8 204

■	1 A	2 K	3 G	4 V	5 L	6 C	7 I	8 W	■	9 H	10 R
■	11 N	12 H	13 U	■	14 U	■	15 J	16 P	17 D	18 V	19 I
20 F	21 E	22 K	■	23 T	24 H	■	25 T	26 J	■	27 W	■
28 W	29 C	30 P	■	31 N	32 W	■	33 T	34 E	35 G	36 M	■
37 S	38 N	39 K	■	40 F	41 V	42 L	43 T	44 Q	45 E	46 R	■
47 B	48 N	49 Q	50 G	■	51 T	52 Q	■	53 T	54 H	■	55 L
56 G	57 C	58 H	59 N	■	60 Q	61 E	■	62 V	■	63 D	64 W
65 L	66 E	67 N	68 V	69 M	70 U	■	71 R	72 G	73 Q	74 O	75 J
76 I	77 S	78 N	79 F	■	80 V	81 W	■	82 R	83 C	84 B	85 T
■	86 N	87 D	■	88 V	89 D	90 O	■	91 P	92 G	93 V	94 K
95 U	96 N	97 T	■	98 U	99 C	100 K	101 I	102 H	103 G	■	104 S
105 D	■	106 Q	107 C	108 E	■	109 G	110 S	111 E	112 P	113 N	114 M
115 T	116 L	117 O	118 I	■	119 T	120 U	■	121 P	122 Q	■	123 N
124 K	125 H	■	126 C	127 S	128 L	129 F	130 E	131 Q	132 B	133 O	134 W
135 V	■	136 T	137 K	■	138 Q	139 K	140 B	141 U	142 J	143 A	■
144 I	145 A	■	146 M	147 N	148 O	149 A	150 T	151 Q	152 S	153 E	154 B
155 K	■	156 H	157 K	■	158 A	159 R	160 I	161 P	162 J	163 B	164 Q
■	165 M	166 A	167 I	■	168 O	169 T	170 E	171 F	■	172 Q	173 L
■	174 R	175 Q	■	176 N	177 E	178 C	179 V	180 H	181 B	182 L	183 T
184 R	185 Q	■	186 F	187 E	■	188 N	189 Q	190 J	191 H	192 V	193 U
194 L	195 P	■	196 T	■	197 P	198 D	199 C	200 Q	201 O	202 L	203 G
204 W	205 B	■	206 F	207 J	■	208 B	209 M	210 E	211 D	212 W	213 T
214 L	215 H	216 A	■	217 Q	218 V	219 N	■	220 S	221 A	222 M	■

No. 1
EMILY DICKINSON: THE SOUL SELECTS

The soul selects her own society,
Then shuts the door;
On her divine majority
Obtrude no more.

Unmoved, she notes the chariot's pausing
At her low gate;
Unmoved, an emperor is kneeling
Upon her mat.

I've known her from an ample nation
Choose one;
Then close the valves of her attention
Like stone.

A	Euphrates	O	To the Orient
B	Mother Machree	P	Heaves to
C	Igloo	Q	Edmund
D	Loaves	R	Seventeen
E	Youth-and-old-age	S	Out of sorts
F	Downtown	T	Upon thine arm
G	Inhuman	U	Lee Marvin
H	Covens	V	Shoo
I	Kenneth Roberts	W	Entrench
J	Items	X	Lover
K	Nieuw Nickerie	Y	Esperanto
L	Shilling	Z	Cajole
M	Oftentimes	Z₁	Theosophy
N	North	Z₂	Shako

No. 2
(MARTIN CARNOY, DEREK SHEARER, (AND RUSSELL RUMBERGER)): A NEW SOCIAL CONTRACT

Almost everyone in America has demanded increased public spending in some form, not only the poor and labor but private business and a middle class demanding better public schooling . . . and more freeways to get from suburbs to downtown.

A	Sind	N	Carver
B	Hods	O	Innocuous
C	Embroiders	P	Adamant
D	Affable	Q	Limned
E	Roving	R	Conning
F	Employed	S	Ornaments
G	Resources	T	Norton
H	Allspice	U	Tombs
I	Naughty Marietta	V	Redoubtable
J	Ebb Tide	W	Animated
K	Whipping boy	X	Cowpens
L	Suds	Y	Tradesmen
M	Oddfellows		

No. 3
(HAROLD J.) KENNEDY: NO PICKLE, NO PERFORMANCE

Summer stock . . . is still a paid vacation. And it does indeed combine the best of both worlds. You have the lakes, the ocean, the swimming, the boating, the tennis, the clear crisp air all during the summer day, and then a baby Broadway at night.

A	Kisser	O	Elgin marbles
B	Elastic	P	Nights
C	Narrow	Q	On the move
D	Named	R	Patties
E	Enation	S	Embody
F	Dim-witted	T	Ruthless
G	Yataghan	U	Filth
H	Nebbish	V	Overdo
I	Oast	W	Rowan
J	Pasha	X	Matte
K	Icebound	Y	Arhythmia
L	Clutched	Z	Nought
M	Kitty	Z₁	Cabbies
N	Leaded	Z₂	Echidna

No. 4
G(EORGE) ORWELL: HOMAGE TO CATALONIA

A porrón is a sort of glass bottle with a . . . spout from which a thin jet . . . spurts out whenever you tip it up; you can thus drink from a distance . . . To my eyes the things were . . . too like bed-bottles, especially when . . . filled with white wine.

A	Growth	M	Enjoined
B	Oistrakh	N	The Witch
C	Ruthful	O	Of eyes
D	Whitewash	P	Cowboy
E	Eldritch	Q	Assiduous
F	Lyre	R	Two-step
G	Lowestoft	S	Attentive
H	Happens	T	Lithe
I	Open-and-shut	U	Optimist
J	Mistake	V	Not on your life
K	Ampere	W	Irenics
L	Grubby	X	At will

No. 5
NORMAN COUSINS: HUMAN OPTIONS

At some point the human race must have its innings. An assessment must ultimately be made in terms of human development. In the end, it is not the nation but humans who will have to account for the record of life on earth.

A Nehemiah
B Other Voices
C Rampant
D Methanol
E Archives
F Ninth
G Carthage
H Other Rooms
I Uvula
J Sweeten
K Intent
L Nodule
M Stated
N Hustled
O Unanimity
P Mallows
Q Abutment
R Nest
S Oman
T Pastiche
U Tootsie
V Imminent
W Offend
X Nimbus
Y Shut off

No. 6
(H. ALLEN) SMITH: BUSKIN' WITH H. ALLEN SMITH

Nobody ever told a good earthy story over a glass of milk. Old Pythagoras once observed that a man is not considered to be thoroughly drunk until, lying flat on the floor, he spreads out his arms and legs to keep himself from dropping any lower.

A Strand
B Moll Flanders
C Indo-European
D Tree
E Hats off!
F Boggled
G Unmoneyed
H Sod
I Knock
J Idiot's Delight
K Nobody's fool
L World so vast
M Ivory gate
N Troy
O Harpy
P Hooker
Q About-face
R Lath
S Lallygag
T Elephantine
U Nurse
V Strengths
W Moved
X Isomorphism
Y Troop
Z Harry

No. 7
DIANE RAVITCH: (THE) TROUBLED CRUSADE

Though it originated in a compromise between officials who wanted to stave off unemployment and veterans' groups that wanted a package of benefits, the GI Bill's most lasting effect was probably its encouragement of the conviction that "everyone, regardless of ability, ought . . . to go to college."

A Everyday
B Infection
C Activity
D New broom
E Enfeeblement
F Raffle off
G Apogee
H Visitation
I In tow
J Tombigbee
K Chases
L Hotsy-totsy
M Tastes woman
N Rootstock
O Orthography
P Upheavals
Q Bootstrap
R Lift-off
S Eschewal
T Dementia
U Colonel
V Reflecting
W Uganda
X Sight gag
Y Agglutinate
Z Demonstration
Z₁ Ever-weeping

No. 8
ERMA BOMBECK: GIANT ECONOMY SIZE

I forgave my husband for not being Paul Newman. Those are the breaks. I realized, being mortal, he couldn't possibly understand my dry skin, boot puddles on my waxed floor, hips that hang like saddlebags, and a house that holds for me all the excitement of a disposal plant.

A Everyday
B Runnymede
C Malapropism
D Andrew Mellon
E Battled
F Outshone
G Moulds
H Bold
I Effusion
J Charts
K Kisses off
L Gabbles
M Ill-fated
N At length
O Nights
P Tousled
Q Ebbing
R Cheating
S Ossa
T Naphtha
U Orthodox
V Meddle
W Yoknapatawpha
X Shrimp
Y In the lead
Z Zuleika Dobson
Z₁ Extraordinary

No. 9
(LOUIS) UNTERMEYER: (THE) PURSUIT OF POETRY

There are . . . countless poems which, if not devoid of rational import, are less meaningful than musical, poems that tend to constitute a kind of poetry as "pure" and meaningless as a beautiful melody or an emotional but abstract painting.

A Ulalume
B Nautical mile
C Tattoo
D Enticement
E Rambunctious
F Managed
G En masse
H Yippies
I Enchant
J Roots for
K Per hour
L Uglified
M Raffish
N Spoon
O Upstanding
P Invention
Q Time bomb
R Oasts
S Floods
T Paladin
U Otter shrew
V Escheat
W Total
X Rankled
Y Ya-ta-ta

No. 10
PHILIP SLATER: WEALTH ADDICTION

The thefts of the poor are obvious . . . But the thefts of the rich are noiseless and unobtrusive. The rich steal from us when they bribe clients or suppliers or government officials and add the cost to the price of their products.

A Partner
B Hefts
C Incipient
D Lithe
E Ichthyic
F Phots
G Soused
H Lobs
I Anchor men
J Tops
K Ether
L Rubs
M Worsts
N Esther
O Affettuoso
P Lover
Q Tiber
R Hitched up
S Affirm
T Deferred
U Debase
V In the light of
W Cavorts
X Torso
Y Inchoate
Z Out of the blue
Z₁ Nervous

No. 11
(DWIGHT) BOLINGER: FIRE IN A WOODEN STOVE

Ask a young child to tell you what dig means, and you are apt to get either a pantomime or an example, "You dig a hole." It takes some sophistication even to talk about easily separable words and come up with definitions or synonyms.

A Beans
B Opportune
C Lash
D Intact
E Nihilist
F Ga-ga
G Eidetic
H Ruche
I Fault
J Imply
K Rules out
L Employ
M It was a dark
N Newton
O And stormy night
P Waste
Q Ommatophore
R Okey-dokey
S Dahoon
T Easy money
U Notable
V Saga
W Toadies
X Oatmeal
Y Vision
Z Expeditious

No. 12
NORMAN W. SCHUR: ENGLISH ENGLISH

A fiddling business is a nickel-and-dime operation, a catch-as-catch-can way of making a living, like street vending or occasional odd jobs. The word is derived from an obsolete slang use of "fiddle": meaning 'sixpence.'

A Not bad
B Oenomel
C Rataplan
D Motivation
E Amalgam
F Nibs
G Weft
H Scows
I Conscience
J Hectic
K Ukase
L Rejoinder
M Eddies
N Nilgai
O Gaff
P Livid
Q Irons
R Seconds
S Hardy
T Existed
U Nodded off
V Ginkgo
W Lacking
X Invaluable
Y Screeds
Z Hispania

No. 13
(JAMES) THURBER:
THE PSYCHOSEMANTICIST
(WILL SEE YOU NOW, MR. THURBER)

I heard an able physiologist who has a radio program say, quite simply, "We do not use up all the food we take in." He wasn't able to get away with that piece of clarity, however. "Ah," cut in his announcer, for the benefit of those unable to understand simplicity, "the utilization factor!"

A Tibia   O Hot potato
B Habitat   P Outwit
C Unhelpful   Q Swee'pea
D Rachmaninoff   R Eisteddfod
E Beautiful   S Malvolio
F Earthenware   T Awlwort
G Rehearsal   U Nowhere
H Telling   V Tarawa
I Hearsay   W Inch by inch
J End of this day's   X Choke
K Pimiento   Y Ichthyology
L Spited   Z Sasses
M Young potato   Z₁ Tourniquet
N Citizen

No. 14
(ALFRED, LORD) TENNYSON:
LADY CLARA VERE DE VERE

From yon blue heavens above us bent
The gardener Adam and his wife
Smile at the claims of long descent.
Howe'er it be, it seems to me,
'Tis only noble to be good.
Kind hearts are more than coronets,
And simple faith than Norman blood.

A Tooth   O Arched
B Epithalamion   P Ratchet
C Nemesis   Q Absent
D Villainous   R Veto
E Eat high off the hog   S Effi Briest
   T Roof
F Anybody's guess   U Emoted
G Laminated   V Damages
H Lips of man   W Edelweiss
I Elaborate   X Valhalla
J Namaycush   Y Edinburgh
K Seabees   Z Ribbing
L Comedy   Z₁ Enthroned

No. 15
STEVE ALLEN:
SCHMOCK-SCHMOCK!

My wife brought home a toy . . . described as "educational" . . . Its brand name is Playskool. . . . I had brought another educational toy . . . the brand name of which is Famus. Some day when my son is going to skool and has become famus for his . . . approach to spelling, he will be thankful we gave him only educational toys.

A Seesaw   M High-and-mighty
B Takes away   N Morbid
C Eustace Diamonds   O On the prowl
D Villainous   P Colorful
E Eat high off the hog   Q Knife
F Anybody's guess   R Sward
G Laminated   S Championship
H Lips of man   T Homily
I Elaborate   U Much Ado About Nothing
J Namaycush   V Out of the ordinary
K Seabees   W Cobblestone
L Comedy   X Know-it-all

No. 16
(W.) SOMERSET MAUGHAM:
CAKES AND ALE

Hypocrisy is the most difficult and nerve-racking vice that any man can pursue; it needs an unceasing vigilance and a rare detachment of spirit. It cannot, like adultery or gluttony, be practiced in spare moments; it is a whole-time job.

A Spirit   N Aesop
B Overbearing   O McCarthy
C Minuit   P Contiguity
D Eccentricity   Q Affront
E Randomly   R Kittiwake
F Slabs   S Earthshine
G Elective   T Senses
H Toucan   U Adjutant
I Midge   V Ninny
J Appointed   W Dice
K Unnatural   X Andromache
L Grief   Y Laves
M Hind   Z Ectoplasm

No. 17
ANNE W(HISTON) SPIRN:
THE GRANITE GARDEN

Releasing a canister of poison gas on a sidewalk is a criminal act, yet those who destroy the emission control devices on their cars, who burn leaded gasoline, who leave their engines running when parked at the curb, are engaged in activities no less irresponsible.

A Arthur Miller   N Goose egg
B Noteworthy   O Raisins
C Needlework   P Aerial
D Each other   Q Noblesse oblige
E Wince   R Intricacies
F Scones   S The view
G Passions   T Euchre
H Insipid   U Geans
I Rataplan   V Alfred Noyes
J Navigable   W Rodomontades
K Taken with   X Dusting
L Hasidic   Y Echinate
M Environs   Z Nestor

No. 18
HOWARD GARDNER:
FRAMES OF MIND

In the Spanish Inquisition, one could receive life imprisonment or even a death sentence if one possessed Arab manuscripts dealing with mathematics: "Mathematicians were denounced as the greatest of all heretics."

A Humble   N Fasten
B Ornithopter   O Reach
C Waves   P Aftermath
D Anchises   Q Meeting
E Rimini   R Entertain
F Descent   S Sweep
G Gasses   T Odalisque
H Amplitude   U Flaccid
I Riotous   V Mines
J Dailies   W In a pinch
K Novice   X Nehemiah
L Encase   Y Dotes
M Rottenstone

No. 19
STEPHEN POTTER:
GAMESMANSHIP

A basic play . . . can be achieved by, say, whistling fidgetingly. . . . I once converted two down into two up when playing golf against . . . the leader of an orchestra, by constantly whistling a phrase from the Dorabella Variation with one note—always the same note—wrong.

A Snowing   N Greedy
B Thalia   O Anything Goes
C Edith Wharton   P Mythology
D Piebald   Q Eccentric
E Honestly   R Sensitive
F East Lynne   S Macao
G Nineveh   T After the Fall
H Pivotal   U Nibbling
I Ottawa   V Sandbags
J Tobacco   W Headway
K Tocsin   X In the worst way
L Edgar Allan Poe   Y Puffin
M Row, Row, Row

No. 20
WALTER LIPPMANN:
THE GOOD SOCIETY

Human beings, however low and abject, are potentially persons. They are made in a different image. And though, as Jan Smuts has said, "Personality is still a growing factor in the universe and is merely in its infancy," it asserts itself and will command respect.

A Wherewithal   O Tiffin
B All's Well   P Hadji
C Lambaste   Q Essence
D That Ends Well   R Gift
E Effort   S Ossining
F Rudiments   T Oboe
G Lanyard   U Dijon
H Incapacitates   V Sights
I Paravane   W Organ
J Panic   X Cess
K Might and main   Y Innate
L Assertive   Z Eleemosynary
M Nimrod   Z₁ Turns up
N Nourish   Z₂ Yesterday

No. 21
OLIVER GOLDSMITH: UPON CRITICISM

Mr. Hogarth used to assert that every one, except the connoisseur, was a judge of painting. The same may be asserted of writing; the public . . . set the . . . piece in the proper point of view; the critic lays his eye close to all its minuteness and condemns or approves in detail.

A Oedipus Rex
B Latches
C Ivory Coast
D Verify
E Esteemed
F Recollect
G Gets on
H Osteopath
I Lord Jim
J Dove
K Shebang
L Masters
M In a pig's eye
N Timber

O Hereditary
P Up in the air
Q Pinches
R Outfit
S New South Wales
T Cope
U Repentant
V Innocent
W Tightwad
X Inhere
Y Caisson
Z In the least
Z₁ Safest
Z₂ Mops up

No. 22
(M. F. K.) FISHER: AS THE LINGO LANGUISHES

Stylish restaurants go through their phases, with beef Wellington and chocolate mousse high in favor one year and strictly for Oskaloosa, Missouri, the next. We need private dining-out guides as well as smart monthly magazines to tell us where we are eating tonight, as well as what we are paying for it.

A Flying Down to
   Rio
B Intuition
C Sweet Sue
D Halation
E Exacted
F Rotten Row
G Assimilate
H Shops
I The base degrees
J Hess
K Every Man in his
   Humour
L Lawless

M In the light of
N Night and day
O Glowworms
P Owl-parrot
Q Lease
R Awestruck
S Niagara Falls
T Glaze
U Up the river
V Ingestion
W Scalawag
X Heteronyms
Y Eternity of thought
Z Shasta

No. 23
(LUDWIG) BEMELMANS: FATHER, DEAR FATHER

There is no good cooking except with garlic – but in the hands of a bad cook it is poisonous. It must be used with extreme care. The most reckless are the English; once they take to cooking with garlic they use it so freely it's impossible even for an Italian to eat it.

A Boxes
B Eirenicon
C Molokai
D Ewers
E Litotes
F Misogynism
G Agoraphobia
H Notwithstanding
I Sheik
J Feistiest
K Accessible
L The scene
M Heed

N Eight
O Richthofen
P Duck-billed
   platypus
Q Eke out
R Axiomatic
S Rootstock
T Foe
U Attention
V The City
W Hewitt
X Enos Slaughter
Y Rotogravure

No. 24
R(ICHARD) HAGEN: THE BIO-SEXUAL FACTOR

If the time between the act of transgression and the punishment is short . . ., if the probability of the punishment given the transgression is quite high . . ., and if the value of the punishment is very negative . . ., punishment will be extremely effective.

A Representative
B Heedless
C Ambush
D Ghastly
E Epistrophe
F Nettlefish
G Tithe
H Hen's teeth
I Entwine
J Buffet
K Intimate
L On the qui vive

M Snobs
N Effendi
O Xerophytic
P Unhinge
Q Almighty
R Letts
S Festive
T Ammunition
U Chiffon
V Thumbs
W Overweening
X Riparian rights

No. 25
(LUIGI) BARZINI: FROM CAESAR TO THE MAFIA

Travelers must be able to feel themselves immersed in the graceful manners and habits of older days . . . They must discover for themselves the quaint local dishes, the pleasant little wines, the homespun cloth, the wisdom, the local handicrafts, the bizarre superstitions.

A Bonds
B Athermancy
C Reluctant
D Zebra finch
E Inspissate
F Newfoundland
G Imbedded
H Fall out
I Resists
J Outright
K Mishmash
L Chortles
M Achilles
N Estivate

O Squibs
P All hell
Q Reformers
R The sheets
S Overview
T The less
U He smelleth
V Elves
W Moth-eaten
X Attitudes
Y Fomented
Z Import
Z₁ Apothecary

No. 26
RICHARD ARMOUR: ENGLISH LIT RELIT

The Graveyard School . . . sat around happily in cemeteries, reading the inscriptions on tombstones, envying the dead, and hoping to see a ghost. . . . A newly opened grave was always a thrill, good for twenty or thirty lines of speculation about skulls, coffins, and worms.

A Raymond
   Chandler
B Investing
C Cashews
D Hogtied
E Apology
F Rioting
G Drop off
H Awash
I Ruffian
J Moppets
K Orestes
L Understand
M Roughly
N Ensign

O New-mown hay
P Gobi
Q Latched
R Inoperative
S Seventy
T Hoad
U Lento
V Intricate
W Topsy
X Roost
Y Enthusiast
Z Losses
Z₁ Ikebana
Z₂ Taylor Caldwell

No. 27
AUSTIN RANNEY: CHANNELS OF POWER

One of the oldest and most persistent beliefs of journalists . . . is the conviction that one of the primary professional obligations of any news medium – indeed, a prime reason for its existence in a free society – is to act as the public's watchdog over government.

A Appropriate
B Unfettered
C Sconces
D Teeming
E Instincts
F Notoriety
G Rififi
H Ambrosia
I Nodus
J Noetic
K Effigies
L Yvetot
M Cosmic
N High Noon

O Amanuensis
P Nesselrode
Q Not so hot
R Elephantine
S Lilt
T Since
U Off the bat
V Floods
W Pajamas
X Overtaxed
Y Wisdom
Z Ethel Waters
Z₁ Rover Boys

No. 28
PHILIP HOWARD: WEASEL WORDS

The delusion that *pristine* is an impressive pseudonym for *new* has become so prevalent . . . that the unhappy word has been stood on its head. By consensus of error it will soon come to mean the opposite of its original and correct meaning.

A Prime
B Heaven
C Ingoldsby
D Legends
E Innocents Abroad
F Pompous
G Haste
H Orphan
I Whimsicality
J Atherton
K Rochester
L Defiant

M Wipes out
N Enchiridion
O Annihilate
P Secession
Q Empyrean
R Loves not
S Worms out
T Osborne
U Room at the Top
V Dust off
W Steeps

No. 29
(WENDELL) BERRY: PEOPLE, LAND, AND COMMUNITY

The tractor has been so destructive ... because it is *unlike* anything else in the agricultural order, and so it breaks the essential harmony. And with the tractor comes dependence on an energy supply that lies not only off the farm but ... outside biological cycles and integrities.

(From *Sierra*, Sept.-Oct. 1983)

A Biscuits
B E Tenebris
C Refractions
D Rose Aylmer
E Year of dearth
F Pinto bean
G Euphrates
H Outright
I Pavan
J Lewis
K Enacted
L Lethal doses
M Accorded
N Niggard
O Dotheboys Hall
P Antlers
Q Netsuke
R Distinct
S Crucial
T One by one
U Militant
V Meres
W Unthinking
X Nettles
Y Insightful
Z Too hot the eye
Z₁ Yucca

No. 30
SEN. WILLIAM PROXMIRE: YOU CAN DO IT!

My father told me about one woman who had suffered from arthritis for many years. She went on a thirty-six-day fast, drank nothing but water, and found that for the first time in years she could move hands, legs, and arms easily and without pain.

A Shoddy
B Enthraldom
C Natatorium
D Worms
E Innards
F Lawyers
G Luffed
H Io
I Angst
J Midst
K Phrased
L Rattan
M Owl
N Xanthous
O Mab
P In white
Q Raffia
R Eurhythmy
S Yesterdays
T Off base
U Unfasten
V Chunky
W Attrition
X Night of fear
Y Dead man
Z On the move
Z₁ Isherwood
Z₂ Threat

No. 31
LOIS DEBAKEY: ENGLISH TODAY: (ARE WE SPEAKING IN TONGUES?)

We no longer converse or discuss; we have *substantive, meaningful, viable dialogues.* A recent *New York Times* headline asked ... seriously: "Will Paris Talks Produce Dialogue?" On the highway a sign announces a low bridge as *impaired vertical clearance.*

(From *The Britannica Book of English Usage*)

A Leverage
B Oswego tea
C In the wind
D Skunks
E Diacritical
F Eardrums
G Barrelhouse
H Averse
I King Oliver
J Epiphonema
K Yearns
L Encomia
M Nuncupative
N Glaring
O La Scala
P Intricacies
Q Swells
R Heavy water
S Tussles
T Oeil-de-boeuf
U Dangles
V A window'd niche
W Young bloods

No. 32
R(ING) LARDNER: MY OWN BEAUTY SECRETS

When dawn comes I always get up and ... try and add a few words to my vocabulary. Like for inst. yesterday morning I put on the following nouns: Wham-Kurtell-Grafe. The first two mean that a caravan is just starting out and the noun *grafe* means that you ain't paid your insurance.

A Raymond Chandler
B Lampas
C Amusement
D Rant
E Dismal
F Nutty
G Efface
H Ruth
I Madras
J Young and foolish
K Out of the ordinary
L Watson
M Nanda Devi
N Bow-Wow strain
O Eat one's heart out
P Awkward Age
Q Unwary
R Tinting
S Yellowplush
T Stuffy
U Etui
V Catastrophe
W Ruining
X Every Jack
Y Sign on

No. 33
(MARTIN L.) GROSS: THE PSYCHOLOGICAL SOCIETY

One of the most successful uses of the insanity law has been to exercise it twice in a row. The person is acquitted of the crime for being insane at the time, then hospitalized for insanity. He is then freed from hospital confinement by proving the opposite: that he is no longer insane.

A Geezer
B Refine
C Offish
D Swithin
E Spent
F The boots
G Horns in
H Ennoblement
I Phoebe
J Shifts
K Yard-of-ale
L Coffin
M Ohmmeter
N Heroines
O Loftiest
P Otherwise
Q Goes to pot
R Incidents
S Chip in
T Athletics
U Lanais
V Sins
W One at a time
X Chews out
Y Insecticide
Z Extravagant quean
Z₁ The pines
Z₂ Youth of primy nature

No. 34
(ROBERT) CLAIBORNE: OUR MARVELOUS (NATIVE) TONGUE

Within a century after Caxton first set up his press, the old, expensive, handwritten book had almost vanished, while its printed successor was becoming almost a necessity for the middle as well as the upper classes. Books, pamphlets, and ... "broadsides" poured from the presses.

A Crawfish
B Listless
C Amphitheatre
D Isis and Osiris
E Bow down
F Obsess
G Resists
H Nickel
I Exacted
J Otter
K Upheld
L Rheims
M Muddies
N Appointments
O Refresh
P Vowels
Q Excessive
R Lays away
S Osteopath
T Under the blossom
U Scaffold
V Topped
W Orchestrates
X Nip and tuck
Y Gab
Z Upper hand
Z₁ Entrhalment

No. 35
AUSTIN RANNEY: CHANNELS OF POWER

Most people who get political information on television get it because they happen to be watching when political information is broadcast. Unlike people who read about politics in newspapers, books, and magazines, they do not get it because they are actively seeking it.

A Annihilate
B Upper case
C Schools
D To boot
E Imbibition
F Night
G Radioing
H Awesome
I Nematode
J Negotiate
K Escalate
L Yelps
M Craig's Wife
N Hiding
O Assize
P Noteworthy
Q Natty Bumppo
R Escape
S Lycanthrope
T Slow boat
U Opinionative
V Flight
W Pickle
X Old Oaken Bucket
Y Whelps
Z Eventuate
Z₁ Repetition

No. 36
G(ROUCHO) MARX: INTRODUCTION TO "WHY A DUCK?"

Trying to keep up with this changing world ... I haven't done too well ... When the Sexual Revolution began, I tried to enlist. But all I got was a series of humiliating rejections. That was from the men. From the women came nothing but hysterical laughter.

A George Williams
B Mulish
C Attention
D Rachel
E Xhosa
F In hot water
G Night Watch
H Twinge
I Replete
J Obvious
K Downs
L Umbrage
M Cost
N Thoth
O Iolanthe
P Outfit
Q North Star
R Tenets
S Oilbird
T Wont
U Henry James
V Youthful
W Alleviate
X Dew
Y Unfeeling
Z Charming
Z₁ Keeping time

No. 37
JACQUES BARZUN: SIMPLE AND DIRECT

The best tone . . . does not talk down or jazz up; it assumes the equality of all readers likely to approach the given subject . . . The plain tone is that of Lincoln always, that of Thoreau, Emerson, William James, Mark Twain, "Mr. Dooley," Fitzgerald, and Hemingway at their best.

A Jimmy Walker	O In store
B Awkward Age	P Moths
C Chant	Q Pennant
D Quetzalcoatl	R Laos
E Usher	S Effleurage
F Epizoon	T Athwart
G Sham	U Nips
H Battle	V Disjointed
I Ajowan	W Dotty
J Royalties	X Ideology
K Zoophilist	Y Revolution
L Ukase	Z Ethel Merman
M Nettled	Z₁ Cattleya
N Shambles	Z₂ The fifth rib

No. 38
NOAH (JONATHAN) JACOBS: NAMING-DAY IN EDEN

Synecdoche degenerates into tapinosis when an invidious or repugnant personal trait is made conspicuous by comparing a person to some base inanimate object which is calculated to detract from his dignity, as *highbrow, egghead, screwball, tightwad, battleax, deadpan, wallflower.*

A Night of the Iguana	M Misstep
	N Irish tweed
B Old Man and the Sea	O Now Voyager
	P Guesses
C Alfresco	Q Derides
D Hobble	R Accolade
E Jerry-built	S Young Man with a Horn
F Abstraction	T Italian Straw Hat
G Cowslip	U Nepotist
H Oxlip	V Edmund Wilson
I Baccarat	W Dog tags
J Spigot	X Ephebi
K Nice	Y Narrow-minded
L Acceptance	

No. 39
MATTHEW ARNOLD: (THE) STUDY OF POETRY

More and more mankind will . . . have to turn to poetry to interpret life for us, to console us, to sustain us. Without poetry, our science will appear incomplete; and most of what passes with us for religion and philosophy will be replaced by poetry.

A Moon	O Tent
B Aldebaran	P Upper crust
C Tiptop	Q Desert
D Thrips	R Yellow Kid
E Holiness	S Opportunity
F Euthenics	T Fort
G Willow	U Outweigh
H Apropos	V Emblems
I Rapacity	W Tiro
J Narrows	X Tiro
K On the off chance	Y Renewal
L Lofts	Z You Made Me Love You
M Distil	
N Sari	

No. 40
GARDNER SOULE: THE LONG TRAIL

While riding horseback, a Plains Indian could shoot from twenty to thirty arrows from his bow, with accuracy, in the same time it took an American, who had to dismount to load his single-shot gun, to get off one shot. Indians won battle after battle.

A Gifted	M Thomas Mann
B Allows	N Hawkshaw
C Rowdydow	O Erstwhile
D Dish out	P Latchkey
E Nobodies	Q Otto Harbach
F Either/Or	R No, No, Nanette
G Roughing It	S Gist
H Stands out	T Twitch
I Oinochoe	U Riffraff
J Unimportant	V Abominations
K Laity	W I Don't Care
L Embolism	X Lattices

No. 41
MARK TWAIN: ELEPHANTS OF LAHORE

The Lahore horses were used to elephants, but they were rapturously afraid of them just the same. It seemed curious. Perhaps the better they know the elephant the more they respect him in that peculiar way. In our own case we are not afraid of dynamite till we get acquainted with it.

A Mutuality	N Heyday of youth
B Apple-pie order	O Awful Truth
C Requisite	P Newer
D Kiowa	Q Thomas James
E The Honest Whore	R Swarthy
F Witchcraft	S On one's high horse
G Attribute	T Fleet Street
H Interminable	U Lute
I Nashe	V Acid test
J Eschewed	W Hecate
K Lure	X Open-hearted
L Enswathe	Y Road map
M Perpetuity	Z Emit

No. 42
PHYLLIS DILLER: THE JOYS OF AGING— (& How to Avoid Them)

I've given a lot of thought to the subject of rejuvenation. . . . I can't keep flying to that island in the Pacific, putting on Adidas and running back and forth across the international date line. It's not making me any younger, and it's giving me calluses.

A Potato	O Haven
B Hardest	P Estaminet
C Yacht	Q Jack Johnson
D Lotto	R Orangutan
E Lighthouse	S Yankee Clipper
F Indian club	T Shiv
G Stiff	U Ostend
H Damn'd	V Fustian
I Insouciant	W Attenuated
J Limbo	X Giving in
K Lacking	Y Iatrogenic
L Event	Z Niggardly
M Retinue	Z₁ Gentian
N Toff	

No. 43
COREY FORD: THE TIME OF LAUGHTER

More than anyone else save Ross himself, Katharine S. and E. B. White were responsible for *The New Yorker's* enormous impact on American letters. Their unerring taste guided it through the formative years, and White's poetry-in-prose because the hallmark of the magazine.

A Cakewalk	N Infamous
B Oedipus	O Monsters
C Rhone	P Embarrassment
D Estimation	Q Otherwise
E Youghal	R Forty-two
F Fabian	S Lamented
G Over There	T Azrael
H Rhinoceros	U Undermine
I Deafen	V Graven images
J The spires	W Heathen
K Healthy	X Ticklish
L Eyebright	Y Enterprise
M The prow	Z Remonstrate

No. 44
EDWARD C. PINKERTON: WORD FOR WORD

"You, sir, are a CAD!" is an old-fashioned expression, but many of us still know what it means. . . . CAD is a shortened form of CAD-DIE, which in . . . Scotland and England meant "a lad who waits about on the lookout for chance employment as a messenger, odd-job-man, etc."

A Extinguished	O Of Thee I Sing
B Defoe	P Newlyweds
C Wallaby	Q Waste Land
D Affluent	R Ommateum
E Rhincodon	S Random
F Drama	T Dacoits
G Counts	U Fasces
H Packs	V Objets
I Inhibits	W Roans
J No use!	X Woodsman
K Kana	Y Ochlocrat
L Election	Z Raphael
M Rhadamanthine	Z₁ Doomsday
N Tondo	

No. 45
(HENRY STEELE) COMMAGER: THE DEFEAT OF AMERICA

The most immoral acts are committed not by hardened criminals but by impeccable gentlemen who preside affably over great corporations, and who sin impersonally and at a great remove in time, in space—and in law—from the consequences of their crimes.

A Canters
B Optimal
C McCoy
D Made fast
E Ambivalent
F Grandiloquent
G Enchiridion
H Revamp
I Tawdry
J Harpoon
K Elect
L Depresses
M Enterprise

N Flimsiest
O Embryonic
P Attend
Q Two fools
R Oswego
S Fetching
T Anchor
U Mealy-mouthed
V Embraceor
W Rambles
X In the main
Y Carbine
Z Amain

No. 46
(JAMES) THURBER: CARPE NOCTEM, IF YOU CAN

Now that practically everybody is rioting around the world, what is to prevent the fifteen million American men and women now sixty-five years old or older from rising up in angry unison and beating the holy bejudas out of television? It is...a comforting thought.

A Tumbledown
B Hounds
C Undertow
D Ready money
E Booby traps
F Exhortatory
G Rachmaninoff
H Civility
I Artist
J Rigmarole
K Pinfeathers
L Enigma
M Ninepins

N Olive Oyl
O Coasting
P Two-fisted
Q Entitle
R Moorhens
S In the light of
T Flowering
U Youghal
V Overdo
W Uninvited
X Cajun
Y Awards
Z Nitti

No. 47
(E. FULLER) TORREY (M.D.): THE ROOTS OF TREASON

Pound had arrayed a scrapbook of Il Duce's dominates our judgments, we often rely on analytic processes when intuitive sensing would be more appropriate (or vice versa). We tend to use the wrong tool for the task.

[Pound had arrayed a scrapbook of Il Duce's... and had published a book comparing him with Thomas Jefferson. ... Mussolini was going to restore the world to greatness, restore Pound himself to the arts to greatness, restore Pound himself to greatness.]

A Took off
B Outstretched
C Ribald
D Ruckus
E Edwin Drood
F Young and sweating
G Torrid
H Hogwash
I Emblems
J Rejoin
K Orestes

L Oppresses
M Tresses
N So as
O Ordaining
P Feller
Q Tea-room
R Roamed
S Epanaphora
T Alembicate
U Spartan
V Of this flesh
W Night Thoughts

No. 48
(BENNETT W.) GOODSPEED: (THE) TAO JONES AVERAGES

By being unaware of which mode of thought dominates our judgments, we often rely on analytic processes when intuitive sensing would be more appropriate (or vice versa). We tend to use the wrong tool for the task.

A Gewgaw
B On the town
C Overfall
D Due
E Stubborn
F Power
G Embow
H Endowment
I Diet
J Tacit
K Aspire
L Oyster
M Journeyman

N Out of style
O No kidding
P Eric
Q Swiftest
R Anthem
S Vicious
T Enthuse
U Roger
V Authorship
W Groove
X Encephalon
Y Sheaf

No. 49
PHILIP HOWARD: WEASEL WORDS

We occasionally . . . say things like "Between you and I." Orson Welles is used to advertise . . . "a sherry for we Amontillado connoisseurs." "I . . . Somebody recently published the sentence: "I refer to he who is known as Shakespeare."

A Poor
B Hormones
C Irish tweed
D Likeable
E Interaction
F Peasants
G Hews
H Old boy
I Wholly
J Anchorite
K Refectory
L Defy

M Weak-kneed
N Entrances
O Assiduously
P Sear
Q Enghien
R Looseness
S Wishbone
T Outlaws
U Reliance
V Devious
W Systems

No. 50
RUTH (SCHWARTZ) COWAN: MORE WORK FOR MOTHER

Men who do housework tend . . . to . . . take out the garbage, . . . mow the lawns, . . . play with children . . . but . . . they do not launder, clean, or cook, nor do they feed, clothe, bathe, or transport children . . . —the most time-consuming activities around the home.

A Routing
B Unadvised
C Throbs
D Hollow
E Clutch
F Ostend
G Wanted
H Attach
I Notched
J Meant
K Ominous
L Righted
M Eucharis

N Wooden
O Ornery
P Rhyparography
Q Know
R Feeble
S Otiose
T Rhomboid
U Motto
V Outwitted
W To match the men
X Hackle
Y Entente
Z Rakehell

No. 51
CHRISTOPHER MARLOWE: DR. FAUSTUS

I am Wrath. I had neither father nor mother; I leapt out of a lion's mouth when I was scarce half an hour old; and ever since I have run up and down the world with this case of rapiers, wounding myself when I had nobody to fight withal. I was born in hell.

A Caudal
B Habitude
C Rhynchocephalian
D Into the highways
E Sun
F Twin Falls
G On the wane
H Pivot
I Howl
J Ems
K Richard
L Moor
M Affair
N Rain

O Linn
P Odd Man Out
Q Wholehearted
R Eos
S Division
T Rabid
U Firth of Forth
V Awash
W Unwell
X Sneer
Y Twine
Z Show white
Z_1 Uther Pendragon

No. 52
(SARA LAWRENCE) LIGHTFOOT: THE GOOD HIGH SCHOOL

During the tumultuous seventies . . . students turned away from math and science and demanded more nontraditional courses. . . . Girls enrolled themselves in auto mechanics and . . . a few daring boys chose to take home economics—long the preserve of . . . girls.

A Leeds
B In view of
C Gluts
D Holiday
E Tendencies
F Furnace
G Open door
H Old men
I Three-ring circus
J Tams
K Homestretch
L Entertains
M Gustavus

N Out of order
O Oeillade
P Deems
Q Havens
R Ignorant
S Gamut
T Hammett
U Suddenness
V Cassowary
W Horace
X Old Nick
Y Ombudsman
Z Lenient

No. 53
T. S. (ELIOT): (Mr.) ELIOT'S SUNDAY MORNING SERVICE

Along the garden-wall the bees
With hairy bellies pass between
The staminate and pistilate,
Blest office of the epicene.
Sweeney shifts from ham to ham
Stirring the water in his bath.
The masters of the subtle schools
Are controversial, polymath.

A Tables
B Shiftless
C Etymon
D Lewisite
E Ihram
F Off base
G Treat
H Senates
I Sweaters
J Ulithi
K Needles
L Dibbles
M Alabama
N Yea-forsooth
O Malta
P On the whole
Q Raphe
R Nepenthe
S Insight
T New birth
U Get off
V Simplistic
W Ethos
X Rattler
Y Vetches
Z Inchworm
Z₁ Cheat
Z₂ Ethnography

No. 54
DICK VAN DYKE: THOSE FUNNY KIDS

A seven-year-old . . . was writing about the news in her life and asked how to spell "knees." Pointing to the girl's knees to make sure that was what she meant, the teacher told her, and the girl wrote, "The brown knees are having a Halloween party."

A Dawes
B Intertwine
C Chest
D Keta
E Vastnesses
F Arthropoda
G Naught
H Dentate
I Yawl
J Know-nothing
K Earthwork
L The hearth
M Heavens
N Orthogonal
O Sawhorse
P Ewe lamb
Q Feral
R Upright
S Nestle
T Nattering
U Yohimbine
V Keepsake
W Ill-will
X Dethrone
Y Seaweed

No. 55
E. Y. HARBURG: (BACK) TO THE DRAWING BOARD

God made the world in six days flat,
On the seventh, He said, "I'll rest,"
So He let the thing into orbit swing,
To give it a dry-run test.
A billion years went by, then He
Took a look at the whirling blob;
His spirits fell, as He shrugged, "Ah, well,
It was only a six-day job."

A Emphasis
B Yokefellows
C Hilts
D Aright
E Rottenest
F Blistered
G Unthinkable
H Rowels
I Glows
J Thorax
K O'Higgins
L Thistle
M Hellions
N Elbows
O Dixieland
P Ribald
Q Aghast
R Whitethroat
S Instantly
T Never-say-die
U Glinted
V By the by
W On the hoof
X Adjoint
Y Right away
Z Devious

No. 56
(JEAN) SHEPHERD: (A) FISTFUL OF FIG NEWTONS

Disneyland could only have been created in America. My country 'tis of thee . . . What is it . . . that makes us create . . Fantasyland, U.S.A.? Nowhere else in the world do they build fake rivers filled with plastic crocodiles and mechanical natives hurling dummy spears at rubber rhinos.

A Switched
B Haunt
C Eclectic
D Palatable
E Howard
F Elderberry wine
G Rehashes
H Dismantle
I Fishy
J Incomparably
K Strum
L Tedious
M Futurity
N Undernourished
O Love-in-a-mist
P Orkney Islands
Q Flan
R Fathomed
S Imbalance
T Groovy
U Naive
V Earache
W Wednesday
X Thales
Y Outstretched
Z Nick
Z₁ Scintilla

No. 57
ESTHER WARNER: THE CROSSING FEE

At my house at the coast, I kept juju under the eaves. There are all sorts of juju. Some protect against one kind of calamity, some against another. At the coast, I needed juju that would "catch" thieves; there were no thefts after the juju was hung in place.

A Eat one's heart out
B Sot
C Tom Jones
D Haw-haw
E Eumenides
F Respectful Prostitute
G Weft
H Adjust
I Reject
J Natterjack
K Euthanasia
L Ruckus
M To hide his head
N Halvah
O Enjoyment
P Cute
Q Rajah
R Ogygian
S Sloe
T Slut
U Ideate
V Nuthatch
W Gavotte
X Faithful
Y Eject
Z Emperor Jones

No. 58
GAVIN YOUNG: SLOW BOATS TO CHINA

The gull seemed to be consciously challenging the bow wave, which only had to rise two centimetres to turn it into a lump of feathers cartwheeling to destruction. . . . Gulls and dolphins like playing games with ships, and both seem to prefer an audience.

A Goneril
B Ash Wednesday
C Villains
D Isotope
E Ne'er-do-well
F Yoruba
G Organdy
H Up to date
I Nocent
J Gems
K Scene
L Let me clutch thee
M On the ball
N Wiles
O Bis
P Outfought
Q Awesome
R Two-fisted
S Scrim
T Thrills
U Opportune
V Clinkers
W Hitched up
X Infighting
Y Night Watch
Z Anathema

No. 59
BOB HOPE: THE LAST CHRISTMAS SHOW

A golf course under the relentless Moroccan sun is a hard par. The fairways were all sand, and every now and then there were little patches of grass. They were the traps. After that match I was so beat I could barely crawl out of my divots.

A Broadsword
B Ornate
C Brewer's
D Howdy Doody
E Open up
F Peter
G Entr'acte
H Thane of Fife
I Hearth
J Eurhythmy
K Lair
L Accrue
M Salem
N Tees
O Cads
P Hester
Q Ravishing
R Intact
S Strew
T Thanatos
U Massage
V Allan-a-Dale
W Scuttle
X Swiftly
Y Hateful
Z Owl's-clover
Z₁ Warren

No. 60
JOHN SIMON: ENGLISH SANS FOOTNOTE

The popular mouth prefers brevity. So monosyllables such as "cop" or "fuzz" will probably outlive such obsolescent disyllables as "copper" and "flatfoot" and the by now archaic "peeler." Slang is like a joke. funny and viable only while it is new.

(From Simon: *Paradigms Lost*)

A Jabberwock
B Olfactory
C Hallows
D Nice-nelly
E Slaver
F Isaiah
G Muses
H Output
I Nullify
J Edwards
K New Hope
L Glance
M Label
N Illicit
O Spook
P Hubbell
Q Spavin
R Apprehensive
S Nize Baby
T Sobs
U Frenzy
V Orpheus
W Oilcloth
X Troops
Y Naysay
Z Odd man out
Z₁ Troll
Z₂ Effects

You could contemplate those long narrow boxes of sparklers gathering dust while you waited for it to be the Fourth of July or Christmas, and noisemakers in the shape of tin frogs for somebody's birthday party you haven't been invited to yet, and see that they were all marvelous.

A Eighty-eight
B Unthought of
C Diota
D Out of this world
E Rakehell
F Anthropoid apes
G Wombats
H Eye-filling
I Liverwurst
J To boot
K Yttrium
L Tavern
M Honesty

N Everywhere
O Cassandra
P Ombudsman
Q Rascality
R Nosebleed
S Expertly
T Rafer Johnson
U Stand-by
V Toasted
W Oath of office
X Rhesus monkey
Y Europe

There is, apparently, something in the air of California, Florida, and other coveted locations that shreds the moral fiber. It is, therefore, only those executives demonstrably impervious to the incidental benefits of Fresno or Fort Lauderdale who get to go there.

A Christopher
B Hathaway
C Athlete's foot
D Roofing nails
E Light meter
F Extended
G Shoddier
H Moocher
I Sobbed
J Moors
K Impotent
L Tone
M Hebetates

N Initially
O Nefertiti
P Shrove
Q Tivoli
R Arrogance
S Necessary evil
T Torrential
U Shiner
V Toodle-oo
W Affected
X Teardrop
Y Unfaithful
Z Suffer

The Elizabethans yakked their heads off over verbal incongruities. Shakespeare created word bumblers like Dogberry, Mistress Quickly, Bottom, the Gravedigger in *Hamlet*. Fielding named one of his characters Mrs. Slipslop, to emphasize her bumbling of our pliant tongue.

A Rogers
B Old Fashioned
C Schmaltz
D Tresses
E Emphatic
F North light
G Razorback
H Oversee
I Mourn
J Esmeralda
K Worry
L Adhesive
M Smirks
N Numbers

O Ticker
P Bought off
Q Upbeat
R Repetitive
S Nature
T Equitable
U Delighted
V Ish Kabibble
W Niggling
X Affenpinscher
Y Dimples
Z Aerolithology
Z₁ Yankeedom

The American housewife . . . on television is depicted as a woman consumed with her own bad breath, rotten coffee, underarm perspiration, and irregularity. . . . In slick magazines, she is . . . brought to task for not trying to "look chic on her way to the labor room."

A Ethereal
B Ruche
C Moon of
   Manakoora
D Ambition
E Burrow
F Oogeny
G Motif
H Bevy
I Earnest
J Christian
K Knut
L Lewis
M Addicts

N Ribwort
O Grinder
P Ephod
Q Euchred out
R Citation
S Omphalos
T Nantes
U Oonts
V Mitigate
W Yorkshire fog
X Swindles
Y In the first place
Z Zachariah
Z₁ Erewhon

Life is a game; we are but players,
Playing the best we know how.
If you are beat, don't let it wrangle;
No one can win all the time.
Sometimes the odds seem dead against you;
What has to be, has to be.
But smile just the same, for life is a game,
And God is a fine referee.

A Leeway
B Aloha Oe
C Roster
D Delight
E Namaste
F Enderby Land
G Right off
H Ambitious
I Newgate
J Dismaying
K Kowtow
L Assure
M Unsuitable

N Feeble
O Moieties
P Aesop's Fables
Q Now's the day
R Jeremiah
S Upside down
T Nighttime
U Escalate
V Meets the ear
W Offbeat
X Oatmeal
Y New thing

Marisa and I decided to call our son Patrick. Our American friends couldn't get over that. They put forth great objections, contending that the child of an Italian girl and a Frenchman couldn't in all decency have such an Irish first name. We hadn't thought of Ireland.

A Jack London
B Echo location
C Arachnid
D Neddy
E Pastiche
F Infiltration
G Embolden
H Ruth
I Recherché
J Enmity
K Avalanche
L Unfulfilled
M Marius
N Orate

O Nether lip
P Tight-fisted
Q Sadat
R Unfolding
S Narrative
T Anchor man
U Natation
V Diggers
W Shunt
X Hafts
Y Accord
Z Drought
Z₁ Occident
Z₂ Watt

We are in for one surprise after another if we can keep at it. We can build structures for human society never seen before, think thoughts never thought before, write music never heard before. Provided we do not kill ourselves, what our species needs most of all is simply a future.

A Letter of the law
B Eleemosynary
C Week in, week out
D Inboard
E Sonic
F Towers
G Heads-up
H Offensive
I Mission
J Affluence
K Suitable
L Lickerish
M Advent
N Truffles

O Euterpe
P Nevers
Q Interfere
R Gobbo
S Hovered
T Tripped
U Trams
V Hush-hush
W Outmaneuver
X Underwent
Y Go for it!
Z Houri
Z₁ Triceratops
Z₂ Scarecrow

Back in the United States, Pound's name was becoming increasingly well known, frequently bracketed with Axis Sally, Tokyo Rose, and William (Lord Haw-Haw) Joyce. . . . Ezra Pound had longed for fame; he had achieved infamy.

A Enlighten
B Fazed
C Upshot
D Launch
E Ludlow
F Ennobled
G Ramadan
H The back
I Owing
J Rack
K Racine
L Ewell
M Yawweed
N Risqué

O Offaly
P Ovid
Q Trajan
R Styx
S Oddment
T Fetching
U The mind
V Radish
W Easy money
X Always
Y Show Me a Rose
Z Okapi
Z₁ Niblick

No. 69
D(AVID) MCCULLOUGH: THE GREAT BRIDGE (AND THE AMERICAN IMAGINATION)

Frank Sinatra sang about the Brooklyn Bridge; Bugs Bunny "sold" it. Its image has been used to peddle everything from sewing machines and cigarettes to Coca-Cola, Kentucky Fried Chicken, fur coats and high-style cowboy boots.

A Dyed-in-the-wool
B Mobsters
C Candide
D Cotter
E Urgent
F Lubbock
G Lancing
H Oscar
I Utgard
J Guy Fawkes
K Hobbits
L Tocsin
M Hocks
N Earth and Sky
O Gage
P Rumpus
Q Egmont
R Alekhine
S Tiffin
T Blanche
U Radiance
V Ivory Coast
W Dobbin
X Gifts
Y Easy on the eyes

No. 70
S.J. PERELMAN: DIAL "H" FOR HEARTBURN

I was so weary of casual, fly-by-night friend-ships—weekends at some joker's in Rowayton that his wife is away in Europe, Ivy Leaguers in madras coats who don't know whether they're in love with their mother or their Porsche—that I just wanted a shoulder to lean on, a home in-stead of a kitchenette.

A Shadowy
B John o' Groat's House
C Powys
D Elementary
E Retentive
F Earth and sky
G Loewi
H Moiseyev
I Astrakhan
J Nitwit
K Doe
L Intimidation
M Athwartships
N Leakey
O Hoot
P Fawn
Q Owens
R Rejoinder
S Hittite
T Esther Waters
U Archilochus
V Rakis
W The Whiff of Grapeshot
X Bawdyhouse
Y Urticaceous
Z Refinement
Z₁ New Holland

No. 71
WILLIE SUTTON: WHERE THE MONEY WAS

The thing that really had the police so confused was that I was using so many different disguises. I would dye my hair different colors; I had side-burns which I could paste on. I could make my eyebrows very heavy by intertwining separate little patches of hair.

A Witticism
B Idly
C Lhasa
D Lithography
E Insist
F Elicit
G Sympathy
H Unto the breach
I Taffy
J Tangy
K Oppressive
L Nadir
M Whittier
N Hedgerows
O Easton
P Riddled
Q Euridice
R The Caine Mutiny
S Hull House
T Ebro
U Make Believe
V Offhand
W Noses
X Edda
Y Youngstown
Z Whirlaway
Z₁ Afford
Z₂ Success

No. 72
ROMBAUER (&) BECKER: JOY OF COOKING

And, if you imagine for a moment that we have triumphantly freed ourselves from the excesses of the Groaning Board, just think of the multi-tude of strange hors d'oeuvre that are downed during a typical big cocktail party in the Age of Anxiety.

A Riveted
B Oregano
C Metaphor
D Ben Nevis
E Amoretti
F U Thant
G Expunge
H Rhapsody
I Buttonholes
J Eagerness
K Cutthroat
L Ketch
M Extremity
N Reaffirm
O Jaunty
P Offstage
Q Youth
R Old Maid
S Fidelity
T Chaffinch
U Ouida
V Overnight
W Kew Gardens
X Islam
Y Natural
Z Goodwife

No. 73
(DON) MARQUIS: THE ALMOST PERFECT STATE

It is possible that when the revolt did occur it was welcomed in other quarters—that is, by the good angels who wished to remain good . . . and at the same time occupy themselves in a strug-gle which took their minds off the thought of eternity.

A Motive
B Arthur
C Rabid
D Quaked
E Uther Pendragon
F Idiot
G Second thoughts
H Twisted
I Hodesh
J Egg
K Anemone
L Lowdown
M Mellows
N Oasis
O Systolic
P Towboat
Q Prometheus
R Ethical
S Revet
T Flit
U Eyesight
V Chow
W Tachometer
X Schist
Y Thither
Z Anthem
Z₁ Tiffin
Z₂ Eighty

No. 74
E. BROOKS WHITE: THE RING OF TIME

The South is the land of the sustained sibilant. Everywhere the letter "s" insinuates itself in the scene—in the murmur* of sea and sand, in the singing shell, in the heat of sun and sky, in the sultriness of the gentle hours, in the siesta, in the stir of birds and insects.
*(Changed from "sound" to get a needed "M")

A Essene
B Butterfly net
C Rin Tin Tin
D Otis
E Outlandish
F Khansamah
G Sites
H Winston
I Househusband
J Interference
K Thinnish
L Esthete
M Thessalian
N High-handed
O Entrust
P Residual
Q Issue
R Night shift
S Guests
T Overrefined
U Featheriness
V Tendon of Achilles
W Insist
X Mettle
Y Ethyl

No. 75
(H. L.) MENCKEN: ON CONNUBIAL BLISS

Marriage is not a contract; it is a way of life. Its essence, when it is sound, is a complete sur-render of many of the natural rights of the in-dividual. It is not comparable to buying an automobile or joining the Elks; it is comparable to entering a monastery or enlisting for war.

A Mah-jongg
B Early Wynn
C Naumachia
D Chiffon
E Kaleidoscopic
F Esparto
G Nefarious
H Ostentation
I Narghile
J Cistern
K Outrageous
L Numismatist
M Nitrate
N Under the Volcano
O Beaters
P Ignominy
Q A grin of bitterness
R Lissome
S Bowdoin
T Limited liability
U Irritate
V State trooper
W Safflower

MAKE YOUR PUZZLE COLLECTION COMPLETE
With Simon & Schuster's Convenient Backlist Order Form

THE ORIGINAL CROSSWORD PUZZLE SERIES

Now in its sixth decade of publication.

Edited by Eugene T. Maleska and John Samson

_____	67987-2	Series 151	$6.95
_____	67988-0	152	$5.95
_____	69519-3	153	$5.95
_____	69520-7	154	$5.95
_____	70638-1	155	$5.95
_____	70639-X	156	$5.95
_____	72351-0	157	$6.95
_____	72352-9	158	$6.95
_____	73161-0	159	$6.95
_____	73162-9	160	$6.95
_____	74047-4	161	$6.95
_____	74048-2	162	$6.95
_____	74915-3	163	$6.95
_____	74916-1	164	$6.95
_____	75848-9	165	$6.95
_____	75849-7	166	$6.99
_____	77849-8	167	$6.99
_____	77850-1	168	$6.99
_____	79178-8	169	$6.99
_____	79179-6	170	$6.99
_____	79787-5	171	$7.00
_____	79798-0	172	$7.00
_____	86408-4	173	$7.50
_____	86409-2	174	$7.50
_____	87194-3	175	$7.50
_____	87195-1	176	$7.50

S&S CROSTICS
by Thomas H. Middleton

Challenging literary wordplay.

_____	72354-5	Series 104	$6.95
_____	74046-6	105	$6.95
_____	74923-4	106	$6.95
_____	77854-4	107	$6.99
_____	79180-X	108	$7.00
_____	86410-6	109	$7.00
_____	87192-7	110	$7.00

CROSTICS TREASURY SERIES
by Thomas H. Middleton

_____	69522-3	Series 1	$6.95
_____	75850-0	2	$6.95

LARGE TYPE CROSSWORDS

Extra-large type that's easy on the eyes.

Edited by Eugene T. Maleska

_____	75826-8	Series 13	$7.95
_____	79181-8	14	$8.00
_____	79780-8	15	$8.00
_____	87218-4	16	$8.00

S&S SUPER CROSSWORD SERIES

A jumbo collection with 225 top-notch puzzles by the experts.

Edited by Margaret Farrar

_____	45690-3	Series 1	$8.95
_____	49436-8	2	$8.95

Edited by Margaret Farrar and Eugene T. Maleska

_____	55754-8	Series 3	$8.95
_____	63302-3	4	$8.95
_____	67592-3	5	$8.95

Edited by Eugene T. Maleska and John M. Samson

_____	72355-3	Series 6	$8.95
_____	79232-6	7	$9.00

S&S SUPER CROSTICS SERIES
by Thomas H. Middleton

A dazzling collection of 185 vintage crostics.

_____	79789-1	Series 2	$9.00

HOOKED ON PUZZLES
by Henry Hook

A satisfying fix for puzzle addicts–dozens of assorted crosswords and word games!

_____	64885-3	Series 2	$7.95
_____	70936-4	5	$8.99
_____	78744-6	6	$9.00

HOOKED ON CRYPTICS
by Henry Hook

A challenging new collection of 55 extra-tricky cryptics.

_____	78740-3	Series 3	$8.00

S&S CRYPTIC CROSSWORD TREASURY SERIES

Tricky wordplay with puzzles selected from out-of-print books.

_____	73511-X	Series 2	$8.99
_____	73512-8	3	$9.00

CROSSWORD TREASURIES

A treasure-mine of puzzling from out-of-print books.

Edited by Eugene T. Maleska, John M. Samson, and Margaret Farrar

_____	64427-0	32	$6.95
_____	66406-9	33	$7.95
_____	68732-8	35	$7.95
_____	74927-7	36	$7.95
_____	87199-4	37	$8.00

S & S DUR-ACROSTICS
by Charles A. Duerr

An exciting series of crostic challenges.

_____	69521-5	Series 6	$7.95

S&S FUN WITH CROSTICS
by Charles A. Duerr

_____	75851-9	Series 4	$7.95
_____	79175-3	5	$7.95
_____	79779-4	6	$8.00
_____	86735-0	7	$8.00

CROSSTALK
by Eugene T. Maleska

Letters to and from America's foremost crossword puzzle authority.

_____	70875-9		$12.00

Send order to **SIMON & SCHUSTER,** Mail Order Department

200 Old Tappan Road, Old Tappan, NJ 07675

Total Costs of All Books Ordered _____

Postage and handling _____

Enclosed is my payment for books ordered _____

New York Residents Add Applicable Sales Tax _____

(Check or Money Order ONLY)

Ship to:

NAME _____

ADDRESS _____

CITY_____ STATE _____ ZIP CODE _____